The Downs from the Sea

"Traffic problems my foot — thank your lucky stars you weren't on the Channel run in mediaeval times!"

The Downs from the Sea

Langstone Harbour to the
Pool of London

David and Joan Hay

EDWARD STANFORD LONDON

Edward Stanford Limited
(A Member of the George Philip Group)
12-14 Long Acre, London WC2E 9LP
First Published 1972
© 1972 David and Joan Hay

Printed in Great Britain by Lowe & Brydon (Printers) Limited

ISBN 540 00965 2

Acknowledgements

The last, and most pleasant, thing one is allowed to do at the end of a book is to say 'thank you' to all those kind friends who have helped us on our way round the coast.

Many aspects of the Kent coast might have been overlooked but for the kindly hospitality and wanderings with our old friends Derek and Elizabeth Russell and in Sussex we enjoyed and profited by the talk and company of Kenneth and Grace Ford of West Wittering. As on other coastal wanderings we are indebted for many a pleasant evening to two of our oldest members of the crew Kip Stafford and Ruth Ure and to Kip for his photograph of the Greenwich Royal Naval College taken on a still May morning after a night passage from the Festival Pier in London. Nearer home it was another old friend and neighbour Max Bryans, who gave us the story of the 'Collar Boy'.

Our warmest thanks are due to Toby Thomson, again at short notice, for nobly standing in and doing the delightful drawings for you and especially our thanks go out to Dennis Mallet for starting each book with one of his delicious drawings.

And finally, because this is the end of a series we would both like to say that we would not have had anything like the fun we did in writing these books were it not for the courtesy and kindly consideration we have had from our publishers on many occasions — 'Thank you' Tony, Peter and Bronwyn, if we are allowed to mention the names of those who direct our modest endeavours.

Contents

Illustrations

Introduction

What better place to complete this series of coastal wanderings than Sussex which was in fact created from the sea. I was born here, at Midhurst behind the downland scarp from which you could reach the sea in the old days down the broad water meads of the canalised Rother to the Arun, at Pulborough and on to Littlehampton with its windmill and old lighthouse on the wooden pier. The canal has long since gone the way of the windmill but the little Rother is still there and you can berth at Littlehampton and run up the beautiful Arun River in your dinghy to the town under the castle.

From Sussex, that land of dew ponds and half forgotten Roman villas, we shall look in to the busy ports of Kent, round North Foreland to the Medway harbours and finish, where we began, in the London river with its time honoured boat yards and bustling quays. But first a word about Sussex itself and the homely line of the South Downs that 'stand along the sea' so charmingly in Hilaire Belloc's poem. No wonder there were once seven busy harbours all at the mouths of rivers, though only four are still on the coast and usable. Even Rye struggling to stay awake in this twentieth century is now well inland.

I find one takes so much for granted on a known and well loved stretch of coast that there is always the danger of overlooking much of its original charm — that is until young, questioning eyes from a new world arrive to jerk us out of our pleasant dwam with questions about things we had taken for granted from birth. It hit us last summer in the shape of the daughter of a Virginian family we have often stayed with over there and I can now tell you a lot more about the Sussex and Kent coast having been made to sit up and think about it.

Poppy, I had better explain, was an intriguing little honey from New York who had written to say, after of course the usual introductory loving flourishes, that she will be 'doing Europe' for the first time and when it is finished she would like to join us on our 'little sail boat and go places'. We gather she has recently graced a friend's fifty foot schooner from Mystic one afternoon and describes the experience as 'cute'. We had just decided to potter peacefully down the Sussex coast and revisit some old haunts instead of the usual summer foreign cruise.

The next thing that happens is an enchanting exchange of letters. Poppy can be severely practical between the bursts of clairvoyancy and besides saying she is arranging another afternoon on the boy friend's schooner 'to get this sailing business wrapped up', she encloses the exact dimensions of each of the suitcases she proposes to bring — 'just in case they don't fit the cabin lockers'! In return I try to convey some flimsy impression of the difference between accommodation potentialities of a twenty-seven foot sloop on a month's cruise and a fifty foot luxury schooner engaged in an afternoon's swan around; especially as there are already three somewhat elderly fuddiduddies and a goddaughter from Oxford to be fitted in with their personal clobber. I even enlarged on the merits of a rucksack or small duffle bag and plenty of warm sweaters. In the event we inspect a dazzling display of minis, bikinis and one tasty little gossamer-like jersey and ruthlessly substitute the loan of a few good East Coast type fishermen's woollies!

But the real *cri de coeur* comes in the postscript. 'It may be a silly question, but please, to be on the safe side, what is the voltage of your ship's electric supply and the plug in points where we hang up! You see, I may have to get some adaptor thing for my hair drier!'

Now, if you have cruised in America you will agree that this is a very natural and practical question coming from a land where you expect to plug in before you have even tended your warps in the Marina. In a few words I attempt to recreate the muddy hard at Bosham or a number of other remote estuaries that are rather favourite haunts of ours. But I give it up and say we can do a 'plug in' aboard at twelve volts. Joan suggests we should reveal our reliance on sun and wind for the job but man-like, I resign myself to a gentler and more apocalyptic approach.

In due course Poppy arrives and we run down to Bosham where we have left *Kala Sona* on a friend's mooring and unload by the old barge quay.

Up till then I suppose we had taken sailing in the estuaries round the East and South coasts and indeed in most European waters rather for granted — rather as a way of life that has become so much a part of us that we have long since ceased to question any of the little inconveniences that become apparent when exposed to the view of a questioning mind from the New World.

Poppy takes one awestruck glance at the antiquated old quay and odd assortment of boats and says,

'Well — wadda ya know?'

To which I find there is really no very logical reply that springs easily to the tongue, so we continue unloading. It was low water and her gaze is concentrated thoughtfully on the quay, now high and dry by some twenty yards of deliciously soft mud.

'Whad's the use of a quay without any water?'

We try to explain about tides and that this is quite normal and in due course — some four or five hours in fact — water will arrive. But it doesn't seem to cut much ice and she wanders off, while we pump up the Avon dinghy which we use on longish trips because we can't stow our proper dinghy comfortably on deck. Poppy returns and goggles in undisguised astonishment.

'Do you haave to do that? I mean, do you reely haave to get aboard in this way?'

We try to explain about dinghies and remote moorings and peaceful estuaries and....but I can see it makes no impression. Poppy is still quite mystified.

'Why can't you go some place else? Some place you can get aboard normally? I mean, do you always get aboard this way?'

She looks thoughtfully down the estuary to where *Kala Sona* is riding peacefully in the afternoon sun. However, in due course, we do ferry all the gear over and after a night down near the entrance we tie up in one of the marinas to pick up crew. Poppy cheers up considerably at the sight of this and even admits,

'Gee, this is reely someth'n!'

In order to catch the tide we have to make a reasonably early start next day and I warn the girls beforehand. We have found by then that Poppy rarely stirs of her own volition, even for early morning tea, before nine or ten, after which there were somewhat lengthy operations on the hair, to remove the night's ironmongery build up and set the scene for the style favoured for that particular day. Even my suggestion that this might present certain problems at an angle of forty-five degrees with a rolling motion added once we got outside, is received with the contempt it deserves.

However, ten minutes of the English Channel on a very choppy morning has an electric effect and Poppy appears in a *recherché* night-gown looking deeply pained and quite incredulously out of the dog house windows.

'What's happened — it's much more uneven here than where I'm used to sailing!'

We explain about the Channel and the North Sea and their little ways and suggest a quick change and breakfast as we are trying to beat a spot of bother coming up Channel. Fortunately Poppy soon cheers up and to everybody's relief positively enjoys the rest of the passage to Littlehampton.

At times Poppy very patiently tried to explain a few relevant facts of life to the less understanding members of the crew but in the main, has now accepted philosophically most of our unfamiliar old world ways in *Kala Sona*. There does remain, however, one almost insuperable problem. Poppy arrives for breakfast wearing her 'brave little girl' expression and toys with her scrambled egg and bacon with one horrified glance at the rest of us tucking into smoked mackerel. (I should explain that all unfilleted fish was out, as she stated firmly, she 'could handle most things — but not those dreadful bones — we don't haave them in the States').

Anyhow I sense a crisis, somehow quite unconnected with the structure of unprocessed fish. With a little encouragement, it comes,

'I got a praablem! The berth is too short!'

Now this defeats me for a few minutes as Poppy's five foot four is ensconced in a normal six foot two berth. Then I remember noticing one night while picking my way gingerly round various bottles, tweezers, double angle mirrors and a pile of odd-shaped lethal pins that Poppy's hair was kind of pyramided at night round several large metal cylinders reminiscent of cheese graters, thus adding some many inches to her natural length. Furthermore, this had to be accommodated on the pillow well clear of the bulkhead.

This was, indeed, a problem and for the time being a solution escapes us. Certain unsympathetic members of the crew suggest an overlap into the chain locker but I have to veto that for obvious reasons.

I don't think it was ever satisfactorily resolved, partly because by the time we arrive at Rye not far away, the real tragedy of the trip is upon us.

One of Poppy's most treasured pieces of yachting equipment was an umbrella in a case that would have done more than justice to the hat of Kipling's Parsee from which, you remember the rays of the sun 'were reflected in more than oriental splendour'. Never before, or for that matter since, has *Kala Sona's* cruising equipment included such an eminently practical, though perhaps unusual piece of equipment. Anyway it goes everywhere with Poppy, just in case! That is, almost everywhere, because now it can't be found and the whole ship is turned inside out to no avail. Poppy is shaken to the wick, even after a stiff gin and Dubonnet or two. She sits in a sort of translucent dwam until suddenly she remembers that though it had undoubtedly gone into the hairdresser's shop at Seaford with her, it had somehow failed to come out again.

Then all hell is let loose; telephones get red hot and letters are dashed off — sadly, all to no avail, partly because, it must be admitted, Poppy is more than a little vague about the name of the shop not to mention the street.

Anyway she is unconsolable and lies for most of the next day which is hot, stretched out on the foredeck, face down in an almost non-existent sun costume, absorbing healing rays on the nether side of her anatomy.

Next day we make for Ramsgate. Poppy is thoroughly enjoying herself and, it must be admitted so are we all, even when it blows up and we have a fairly rough passage into a force five/six wind almost heading us and producing slab-sided waves. In fact the rougher it is the more Poppy beams and exudes *bonhomie*. It is only in port that we seem to stagger from crisis to crisis.

The weathercast for next day is good and we toy with the idea of showing Poppy the Thames estuary and the boats coming in down the five channels. But she has decided with tears in her eyes that once again Paris calls and we decide to take her over to Calais and dump her on the train instead. As soon as the gates are open we lock in to the *Bassin l'Ouest* and the girls go off to choose a cafe for the evening meal.

Over coffee and cognac we have an enthusiastic, if one sided, discussion on literature as a mirror on contemporary life. Poppy has a catholic if somewhat uncertain acquaintance with a wide range of modern authors most of whom we, not being with it, have to plead ignorance of and she happily hoses us down with meaningful summaries of their significance in the modern life rhythm of the New World. The *Reader's Digest* has certainly left its mark on the new society and is at its most colourful when regurgitated with a disarmingly bright apocalyptic kind of child-like simplicity. We gather that the life rhythm of the subsensory perception is all-important. Our 'has been' generation is not forgotten and graciously,

'We have', Poppy announces thoughtfully, 'also, great social writers of the past like Angela Thirkell, and....and' (after a desperate pause) 'Jane Austen, who have added a whole range of meaningful thoughts to our awareness.'

We admit to a nodding acquaintance, even in England, with these authorities but feel constrained in passing to add that, perhaps, we would never have thought of mentioning the last two in the same breath. Poppy is enchanted that we know about them and sweeps us on encouragingly towards a sea of *avant-garde* paperbacks — some of which I have seen adorning the crevices above her bunk.

Next morning we duly decant her and her belongings at the railway station with mutual expressions of goodwill. It has been an experience — for both of us. And funnily enough I think Poppy is really genuine when she forces back a tear bravely and says she has enjoyed every minute on 'the little sail boat'.

'It sure is like leaving home a second time — an' we certainly got around a bit didn't we?'

She says 'hi' rather uncertainly and disappears into the compartment as the train moves off.

We return aboard and have a long drink. It is unnaturally quiet at first but I dare say in a short time things will assume their old familiar rhythm and tomorrow we shall be on our way again.

But I can't help having a sneaking suspicion that there will be moments when we shall think of Poppy almost with a sort of nostalgic affection, battling bravely with life on a little English sail boat armed only with an umbrella, a hair drier and a hopeful assortment of bikinis.

But we must return to Sussex for a moment and just have a few more serious words about it before we take you up the coast on what I hope will be, if not more 'meaningful', at least a more peaceful trip.

Both Sussex and Kent have had a very lively past mainly because, I suppose, the open beaches of Sussex were a Godsend to all the early invaders, including the Romans, though even for them communication both eastwards and westwards wasn't very easy because they were cut off by huge undrained marshes which are still here today, round Rye on the east and the Chichester waterways to the west. To the north of course was the great tangle of forest land on the soggy clay of The Weald which made communications with London extremely difficult until roads were cut through it. Then in late Tudor times the Sussex iron industry got rid of most of the woods, which were felled to provide fuel for smelting and so we have

The 'Medway Queen' – once a familiar sight on the Kent coast.

the downlands and the rich farmlands we know today.

I think the saving grace of Sussex has been that man has fortunately collected most of his surburban sprawl into areas like Brighton, Eastbourne and Worthing along the coast – places which are quite useless to sailormen and happily they have left the little ports of Newhaven, Littlehampton and Rye to those who still enjoy the sea. If you want to go inland there are still largely untouched villages like Burpham which is half clustered and half strung out in a sweep across the Arun meads and is of a sedate country comeliness. Amberley has now become rather an artists' colony but Petworth, Midhurst and Lindfield remain much as they were, looking rather like overgrown villages in which the houses are generously spaced and constructed with bow windows, overhangs, porches, cosy cornices and grey and rosy red brick mixing with green shutters and tiles. At Horsham you have stone roofs, fishtail tile hanging and rich but restrained timbering. Much of the cottages are still white weatherboarding and even thatch is still being carried out and repaired over large areas. So why not sail in and enjoy it? You can still take your dinghy up many of the rivers which mark the old divisions — Rapes the Normans called them — and go up not only past the history but through the meadows and river banks bright with viper's bugloss, nightshade, sea pinks, speedwell, sainfoin and share the little byways with the Brent geese and wild duck as they come in towards evening for shelter.

As to your first sight of Sussex from the sea — that is a bit more difficult to describe. One thinks in terms of the blue line of shore when approaching the West Country from Brittany, or the vivid green of the Isle of Wight as first seen en route from the Channel Islands. I think that after seeing Sussex from a distance and then gradually closing, you will be left inevitably with a lasting sensation of an infinite range of shades of brown. I like brown; it is a most warm and cosy and all embracing colour. There is not only the brown of the woods, of which there are almost endless shades, but the golden brown of bracken in autumn, the dark brown of the pines and the chocolate loam of the fields in certain parts of The Weald. The great cart horses on the farms when I was a boy used to be in wonderful shades of brown and in all I think it is the colour that goes furthest back in time and thought — perhaps even to the primeval twilight of the first toil of man on a hitherto undisturbed earth. Against this rich backcloth the blaze of the autumn colours or the bright golden flashes of the primroses, coltsfoot and cowslips in early spring show up to perfection.

Anyway let us go into Langstone Harbour as the first on our trip eastwards and even here it is still possible to remember that one is stepping ashore in an ancient land.

The Old Quay at Emsworth.

Bosham Quay at low water.

Bosham Church and Village across the creek.

Birdham Pool has now been converted into a modern marina.

Langstone Harbour

I couldn't, even after the most delicious orgy, call Langstone attractive but like one's mother-in-law it has its uses. I know it was once the Port of Havant with its own Customs officials, and until the end of the nineteenth century, still in use as a coasting port, but I'm afraid I still find it depressing. It includes a fine sheet of water — though you are apt to take a few barnacles off near low tide — but the western side is too heavily built up and the back side of Portsmouth, which you are looking at, is not its best feature. The best place to try and stay afloat within reach of the shore, is on the Hayling Island side at the lower end near Lake Sinah and it's a queer place. The joys of civilisation here, include the ferry, the harbour master's office and a club house. There is also fortunately the *Ferry Boat Inn* where you get a warm welcome, hot pies, freshly cut sandwiches and can sit in comfort while you watch other poor folk coming in and wondering where to hitch up for the night, and that is about it. On the seaward side, the golf course is fringed with soft sand and gorse bushes, while the marshes surrounding Lake Sinah are cluttered up with the most extraordinary collection of derelict barges, houseboats and landing craft that I have ever seen. Provisioning is a bit of a problem, you either walk half a mile or so along a rather dusty road cut through the scrub to the outskirts of suburbia and then a further mile and a half through this built up area to reach the shops or you must hope the Portsmouth Ferry is running.

Despite these rather unpromising first impressions it is worth looking in, if only to sail up to the old village of Langstone on the mainland if the tide is right and visit *The Ship,* an attractive long whitewashed building and the headquarters of the Langstone Sailing Club. If you hit a day when the water skiers are out, it can be a thought noisy up here, for a section of this area has been allocated to them, but there is plenty of room for everyone and, if you are a bird watcher, you will find the upper part of this harbour, with its wide mud flats and marshes not unattractive – especially in the late autumn, if you are still afloat, because this is a favourite winter resort for the dark breasted Brent geese when they decide that Siberia is getting a bit too chilly.

At Langstone you will see the channel leading enticingly through the bridge towards Emsworth, but alas this way is now only open to small motor boats with less than seven foot headroom. Until 1823 Hayling Island really was an island which could be cut off for days when gales whipped up the waters of its treacherous creek. Then a long, narrow, rickety bridge was built, supported on wooden piles, to be supplemented later by a railway bridge across which an enchanting little train puffed backwards and forwards from Havant Station to the southern part of the Island. Now of course Hayling, as befits a sophisticated resort, is hitched to the mainland by a great wide highway, but at least the water is still allowed to flow under this bridge, and a small boat can get through. In the north western corner there is no longer any connection between Langstone and Portsmouth harbours.

Not even the most doting native could call Langstone cosy. But this has one advantage in that it is less popular and crowded than others along this part of the coast and though it has a bar, there is considerably more water than over the Chichester entrance, so it is available for much longer on each tide – well, there we are, it's all yours any time you want!

Chichester Harbour

Chichester next door is a very different proposition. The bar of course can be unpleasant in a strong on-shore wind and it is often a race with the tide to get in and back to the home mooring on a Sunday evening. But, as a dinghy sailing area, or even gentle pottering when the weather shuts down outside, it is splendid, with four separate creeks to explore. You may have to do more motoring than sailing up some of these channels because, inevitably, moorings are creeping down them, but wherever you go you will be in unspoilt country with the line of the South Downs in the background. My favourite anchorage, if the wind is right is at East End in the Chichester Channel, off the steep-to shingle beach, because from here there is a sense of space away northwards to Bow Hill and the Trundle on the far ridge. I am afraid other people think so too, which means a bit of a crowd especially at weekends, because apart from dinghies locally based yachts tend to motor downstream for picnics on the shingle.

Emsworth Channel

We used to put in here for the night when on passage but there is no reason why you shouldn't stay and explore the possibilities; so, for our first day's potterage we might go up to Emsworth. The east side of Hayling Island always looks a great deal more attractive than the west with its two long creeks, Mengham Rythe and Mill Rythe. If you can find room to anchor or a vacant mooring in the former you will be able to enjoy the hospitality of the Hayling Island Sailing Club — that is if you haven't gone aground in the process of dodging moorings in the middle of the channel. Mill Rythe is marked by perches but dries out, so if you want to stay you will either have to take the ground or berth at one of the yards up the creek. From here it is only about half a mile to *The Maypole* and to the shops at Stoke.

Both these creeks are possibilities for a night. By day, however it is much more fun to take the tide up to Emsworth and lie against the old quay at high water. From there it is a short walk to the Square with its Georgian houses and, indeed, I know of few places where you slip so quickly from the eighteenth century to the modern day, for just beyond the top of the Square runs the busy main road to Fareham. Yet half a mile away at the quay you are quite unconscious of the traffic noises which disturb neither the old barnacled jetties nor the ghosts of the barques, carracks and sailing barges which warped into the berths a few centuries ago when Emsworth handled most of the traffic for the Port of Chichester. On a more mundane note, this is one of the most convenient places I know for shopping by boat, because you have all the facilities of a large town within a short walk from the quay, but you will have to keep an eye on the tide and find deeper water soon after it turns.

If you want to spend the night nearby you have two possibilities. You may find room to anchor below the moorings, or if your draught is not above four feet I suggest you try the new Marina on the east side. I found Captain Henry very helpful and I am sure you will be comfortable there even if it is not very picturesque. Inside the banks of the Marina you have modern yachts and motor boats all stacked away neatly on their pontoons. Yet what I like about the place is that you have only to climb these banks to look out, when the tide is low, over an area of marshy flats, which are as still and silent, except for the calls of the seabirds, as they were hundreds of years ago. I suppose it has something to do with the failing light and the little boats lying over at odd angles and the derelict hulks which thrust a rather sinister black outline into the sky — but it adds up to a pleasant sense of unreality and timelessness.

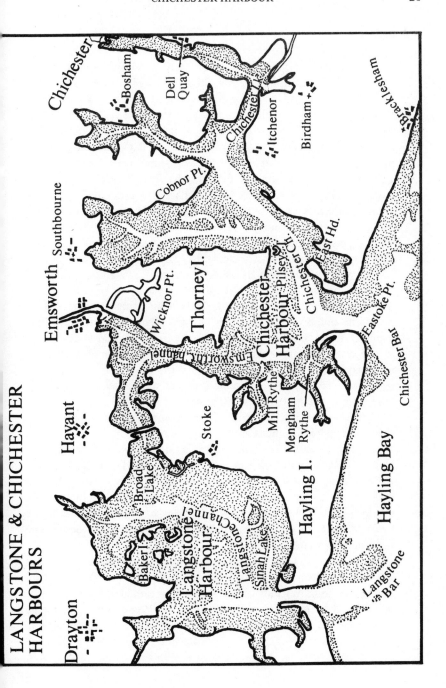

LANGSTONE & CHICHESTER HARBOURS

Bosham

There is not much to send one into a delirium of excitement up the Thorney Channel unless you want a church or an R.A.F. base, so, unless you have a 'make do and mend' day for which I find Chichester Harbour eminently suitable, I suggest a visit to Bosham — which really is a honey of a place, I think you will agree. It has survived a long history, at least from Roman days, but I suppose its main claims to fame are connected with three men. I am sure you will know all about the last two but the first, Father Dicuil, was a quite fascinating Irish monk who managed to establish a Christian church here, making his home in a little cell which can still be seen and living a solitary and precarious life until joined by three or four others. This was two hundred years before Augustine landed in Kent and it seems doubtful whether this early church survived, for St Wilfrid who will probably insist on a mention as we pass Selsey Bill in a page or two, had a very rough reception in the seventh century when he first attempted to let a little light into these parts. These early Irish monks were real toughies and first class seamen, sailing regularly to Iceland in their little twenty-one foot skin boats where, as one charmingly puts it, 'there is so much light at midnight that a man may see to pick the lice from his shirt'. After this, the establishing of an early church in a remote corner of heathen Sussex would have seemed like a bus ride to Brighton.

The second character to whom Bosham claims a proprietory right is our old friend Canute. Yes, you have guessed — this is another of the spots where he did his famous act with the waves. But here at least its popularity as a Danish stronghold is irrefutable and the historians seem to be agreed that Canute actually lived at Bosham long enough to have a daughter who died aged about eight, and was buried in the Church, the evidence being a stone coffin with the bones of a child which was found in the right place about one thousand years later.

The Danes, I may say, could hardly be described as peaceful settlers in Bosham, on one raid taking a fancy to the bells of Bosham Church. In some versions of the story they carried them all away — in others they restricted themselves to the largest. But you will be glad to hear that they didn't get away with it, for the bells were so heavy that the ship sank — just outside the harbour. Now, when the Church bells ring, the bells or bell at the bottom of the Channel join in in sympathy – specially for yachtsmen!

Finally, as I'm sure you will remember, it was from Bosham that Harold set out on his ill fated 'peace in our time' visit to Normandy when he gave William the excuse for claiming that the Kingdom had been pledged. Bosham Church duly appears in the Bayeux tapestry and indeed, with its Saxon as well as Norman bits – not to mention the Roman stones embedded in its walls – is still well worth a visit.

In fact the tapestry is also worth a visit because the Norman ladies seem to have had a soft spot for Harold and given him a lot of space. As *Dux Angelorum* we see him and his bodyguard riding to the Church at Bosham on the most unlikely horses (anatomically) and to the most inadequate ecclesiastical edifice. Then we see him with a friend entering on bended knee to offer prayers for his safe passage. After which they go to the Manor House, like sensible fellows, for a good party before the cruise – as you probably remember this belonged to his Pa, Earl Godwin, as indeed did the whole of the village. Farther on, a messenger is depicted summoning them to their ships in Bosham harbour and – such a homely touch across the ages – there is no more water at low tide than there is now, so you see them, having stripped off their lower garments, paddling across the mud to their boats carrying their dogs under their arms. Then the last picture of the 'clip' shows them under full sail – to disaster.

You will in any case be conscious of this Church as you sail up the creek to the old, high quay. The village lies in a semi circle round the head of the starboard creek and right down to the water's edge. At low water the mud flats are covered with a bright weed that makes the whole area look like one gigantic village green. Boats and cars live happily side by side here, for the boats may be sitting on the mud flats right at the edge of the road where you park your car. Indeed I must own up to one time when I left my own car a bit too long and was only too glad to have a dinghy handy to row out to it. The great saving grace of a good vintage car is that it stands high in the water and even though it was over the running boards I was able to drive off quite happily – towing the dinghy behind, until it grounded. Modern cars might not take quite so happily to the nautical life.

Well, goodbye Bosham for the moment, because I have to admit to a faint nostalgic drool every time I revisit it whether by

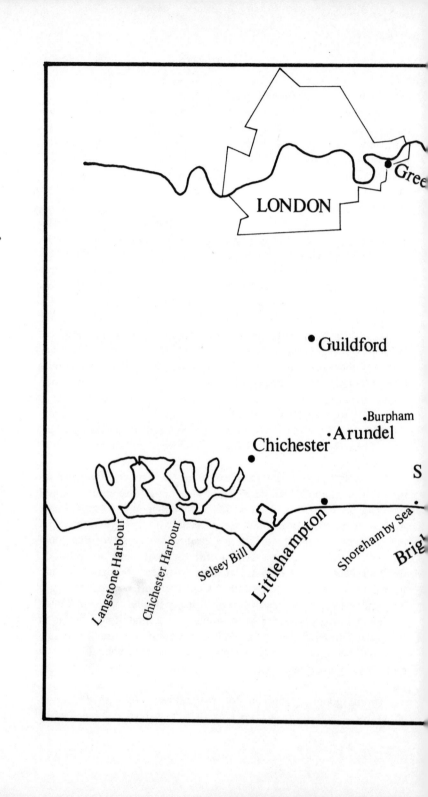

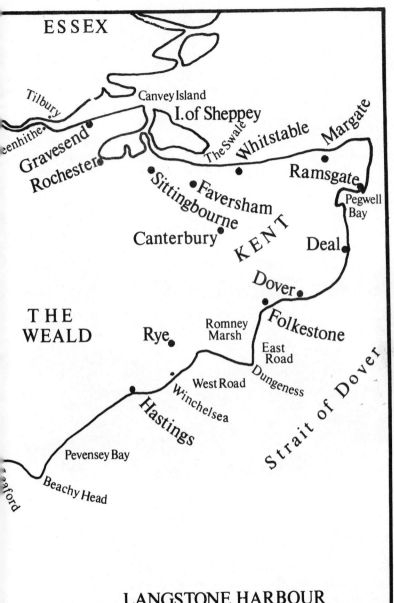

ESSEX

Tilbury

Canvey Island

I. of Sheppey

eenhithe

Gravesend

Rochester

The Swale

Whitstable

Margate

Ramsgate

Pegwell Bay

Sittingbourne

Faversham

KENT

Canterbury

Deal

Dover

Romney Marsh

Folkestone

THE WEALD

Rye

East Road

Dungeness

Strait of Dover

West Road

Winchelsea

Hastings

Pevensey Bay

Beachy Head

aford

LANGSTONE HARBOUR
TO THE POOL OF LONDON

land or water. I have known it since a child and it will always represent all that is most cosy and exciting and yet snug in Sussex. The coming and going of ever increasing numbers of yachtsmen and dinghy sailors hasn't broken the charm — any more than the drunken parties of legionaires from Vespasian's camp nearby did in the days of the Roman occupation. It is high time I stopped sitting on the wall by the old mill and rowed back to *Kala Sona* before the ebb loses its punch. Bosham at high tide is cosy and comfortable like a Dutch housewife but after the ebb I must admit a certain amount of the comfort drains away between the derelicts and the stranded dinghies.

The channel from 'The Ship', Itchenor.

Itchenor

Again, the same little problem — unless you have legs, I am afraid it is unlikely that you will find a mooring or place to anchor anywhere near Bosham, so thick are the moorings here. The best bet is to make for Itchenor and get the harbour master to fix you up. They have a very sensible arrangement there, a visitor's buoy which you can pick up free for a short time while you go and ask for a mooring, but it will cost you the earth if you try to stay there for

too long! It is a Godsend to the visitor and protects the local mooring owner at the same time. I wish all places would follow suit!
Itchenor nowadays is a mass of moorings, but that doesn't detract
from the charm of this little village with its pleasant street of whitewashed houses and its Church with a rather gnome like tower. Once a
considerable centre for boat building, it is I feel, quite in character
that it should have a chandlery but no other shop of any kind. But
not to worry — the landlord of *The Ship* seems to be able to lay his
hands on anything a wilting sailor can want! And after what you will
agree is one of the best meals you have had at a very reasonable price
you can join in the local gossip at the bar and feel really at home.

Chichester Channel

Any large area of sheltered water will nowadays attract its fleet
of boats, particularly when it is as close to London as Chichester
harbour. Though we have mentioned congestion of moorings up some
of the channels, the Chichester authorities have actually done better
than many others in preserving enough open water to permit the
possibility of sailing within the harbour area. If you will come with
me up to Chichester Lake we can see how the number of boats in
this area have been tucked away in yacht basins so that they are not
occupying valuable sailing space when not in use.

The channel up to these basins is well marked, but even before
we reach the first, Birdham Pool, it dries out so we have to watch
our tides. This Pool is, I suppose, one of the oldest marinas in the
country, providing sheltered moorings in a delightful tree lined basin
long before the rather unattractive name, marina, had come into use.
As late as 1909 Frank Cowper could write of entering the Chichester
Canal through Birdham Lock and going right up to the town to lie
afloat in 'a very quiet, clean berth' near the railway station. At one
time indeed it was possible to go right from the Thames to Portsmouth by canal, the Chichester canal being an important link in the
system. Now of course Birdham Pool has had to bring itself up to
date with pontoons and stagings, but it is still an attractive spot
which reminds me a little of the *Lystbadhavn* in Copenhagen.

The Chichester canal is no longer navigable, but its first reach is
still in use, with a few boats and houseboats which look rather like
old College barges, moored among the reeds and waterlilies where the

moorhen scuttle about undisturbed. Here again you get one of these Chichester harbour contrasts. This quiet, overgrown stretch of canal lies on one side of a road; and on the other is one of the newest and most sophisticated marinas, with club premises, shops for food and clothing, piped water and electricity, showers and toilets, chandlery, boatyard and space for nine hundred yachts of sizes up to eighty feet. The layout of the pontoons is spacious, almost up to American standards, for across the Atlantic yachtsmen are not expected to cope

Dell Quay, the old port for Chichester.

with the awkward manoeuvres required in some of our yacht harbours when turning in a narrow space. In any case, manoeuvres of this type would not be possible in a country where you aim to plug into the electricity before bothering to tie up.

The dredged channel up to the Yacht Basin is marked by beacons, but it is narrow and occasionally on a Sunday evening when the procession is returning from a weekend away, someone will clot it and go aground. This normally blocks the channel completely and, on a falling tide, creates chaos as yachtsmen all the way down the queue are faced with the alternatives of abandoning ship or arriving very late in the office next morning. However, it is all part of the service and next day the deserted boats are collected and tucked away in their proper holes.

Before we leave Chichester Lake there is one more spot to visit. About a mile up river, you will be surprised to find a high and impressive quay. This, Dell Quay, is another place which was at one time the Port of Chichester. There is still a shipyard up here and a perfectly possible mooring for a boat which can take the ground. If I had the right sort of boat I would certainly choose to moor here, for it is one of the most peaceful and delightful spots in the whole area, with a few little houses up the one street, a comfortable Sailing Club and an excellent pub, the *Crown and Anchor*. What more can you want, except water to float in?

Round Selsey Bill
to Beachy Head

Going east, I think the best time to leave Chichester harbour is about an hour after high water. On a falling tide this still gives you plenty of water over the Bar and though you will have about two hours of adverse tide, it is never strong in Bracklesham Bay. By the time you reach the much stronger tides round Selsey Bill the east going stream should have started, that at least is the theory and I must say it seems to work on the rare occasions when the tides play the game according to the book!

Most of us would choose the middle passage round the Bill and through The Looe. The inshore passage may dodge the tides but is, to my mind, only safe for locals, while the passage outside the Owers is a long way round. I would only suggest it in really bad visibility.

As we sail, leaving the R.W. chequered buoy to starboard, there is again time to remember that this area round Selsey Bill is one which has seen much change within the last few hundred years. Somewhere under the sea is the site of the first Cathedral and monastery in Sussex, built by St Wilfrid in the seventh century. Since his abortive attempt to land at Bosham he had learnt a thing or two about tactics. He started his adventures hereaways by going aground in a gale. This of course was a wonderful opportunity for the heathen to attack and wipe them out and it took many prayers and a stone thrown, David style, at the chief priest, not to mention some hard fighting, for the small boatload of one hundred and twenty Christians to survive the first attack. Then Wilfrid tried a few more prayers and took a leaf out of Moses' book by arranging for the tide to come back an hour early, so that the ship floated and sailed away just before the fourth attack, under the leadership of the King himself, really got organised. This evidence of divine intervention did not however immediately make Wilfrid acceptable so he seems to have arranged next for a drought, with its accompanying famine, having cunningly discovered that the natives did not even know how to fish. The rest was easy; he taught them how to fish and make the appropriate nets and they were in the bag.

The reasons for the transfer of the See to Chichester in 1075 are not entirely clear — maybe it was already too close to the sea for comfort. Nor am I clear why poor old Wilfrid should have been replaced by Richard as the patron saint of the local Cathedral, leaving only a little Chapel to remember him by, to the north east of Selsey Bill. Here one stormy Christmas night the priest found himself saying Mass for the sheep, cows and a donkey, the only part of his congregation that answered the call to midnight mass.

By now we should be past the Bill and sailing over The Park. This is no fictitious name; only about four hundred years ago it was a great deer park, a favourite hunting ground for English Kings. It is now equally popular with local fishermen, judging by the number of lobster pots around to catch in a poor yachtsman's propellor. Pagham Harbour opposite The Park is of course no harbour, only an area of marshland, so our first possibility for a night's harbourage is in Littlehampton, still a few miles further on.

Littlehampton

Chichester to Littlehampton is one of these awkward little cruises where there is a bar at both ends and two tides may be needed to achieve a passage of only about fifteen miles. If you are a shallow enough draught to get over both bars near half tide you should be able to manage it on one tide, but this will be easier going west because of the timing of the off-shore tidal streams.

I don't care how many days I spend in port here — don't believe the rumours that it is now stuffed with retired politicians sunning themselves! If you don't instantly fall under the spell of the little port with its fairground and wooden pier, well, take a turn up the enchanting River Arun in your dinghy and enjoy the lush meadows, wild flowers and great castle jutting out of its woods above the bend of the river. If by the time you have got to the *Black Rabbit* you still aren't 'turned on' there must be something wrong with one of us.

It reminds me faintly of Dieppe across the channel, with its lawns and flower beds, both have sea beaches but Dieppe lacks the river and interesting hinterland. And you can still see tamarisk hedges growing naturally and there are poppies in the banks. My greatest joy as a small boy, was to be allowed to spend a day and sometimes part the night with the Harbour Master in his little launch — how well I remember its old Kelvin engine which seemed to go thunk, thunk all day. It hardly seemed to notice whether it was in gear or not and you started it by setting the handle a bit above the floor and jumping on it till something happened — which it always did eventually. We would potter about on pier or dock inspection and then push off over the bar out to sea to meet a Scandinavian timber boat or general coaster, to pilot them in and berth them alongside the town quays. The greatest fun was when, weather permitting, they came in late evening or even at night. There were very few yachts in those days.

There were a lot of quaint local sayings, I remember, such as, 'Winkles eaten in March are as good as a dose of salts'. Don't ask me why. Anyway Littlehampton was fun, I mean, where else outside Holland could you enjoy a windmill, a wooden pier and a pub all in one spot — oh, and a Saxon cemetery thrown in for good measure — only the windmill is no more, but in compensation there is a variety of pubs to choose from — the *Kings Arms, Ship and Anchor, Britannia, Nelson* and *Locomotive* will all welcome you; if you want a meal I should try the *White Hart*.

There is a glorious country of beech woods and breezy downs and rich meadows just beyond the town's back yard. It must have been a pleasant land in the Bronze and Iron ages — until those 'time and motion study' gents, the Romans, came and tidied it up. To those practical business men the Downs were merely ready made earth works. They took one look at this orderly row of hills and, being compulsive builders of forts, roads and villas they peppered the whole countryside from here to Sandwich with their unimaginative crudities. There being no amenity societies in those days or planning restrictions, they let rip and at least left enough debris to provide an army of archaeologists with their bread and butter for centuries to come.

To Gilbert White the Downs were the haunt of all the wild life he loved so dearly and recorded so painstakingly. To cricketers the

Littlehampton today.

The main harbour at Rye is now two miles from the town.

Rye was originally built on an island.

Mermaid Street, Rye.

Arundel area will recall Richard Newland — the father of the game. He was born here and made eighty-eight for England against Kent as long ago as 1745 — quite undisturbed by the news that Bonnie Prince Charlie's invasion had got as far as Derby — what a nice sense of first things first! Similarly in 1812 'The Gentlemen of The Weald', unde-terred by Napoleon's invasion barges across the water, met 'The Gentlemen of the Sea' for one hundred guineas and walloped them by seven runs. Furthermore, I'll bet you didn't know that women's

Littlehampton 1909 — the windmill is now a helterskelter.

cricket also blossomed in the eighteenth century! Not to be outdone by Women's Lib. movements of nearly two hundred years later, the married women challenged the unmarrieds in 1796 at Bury and slaughtered them by eighty runs. After this there was no holding them and they challenged and beat 'The Rest of England'. I would hazard a guess that they were quite unlivable with for a year or two!

I may say the spirit of Sussex needle matches is not dead. I well remember that delightful friend of cricket, Sir Learie Constantine recalling a local Sunday match at a well known country house in Sussex in which the 'current' Test cricketers had been

c

invited to play. The local Vicar, a man of firm ideas and muscular Christianity was umpiring and Larwood had been told to remember it was Sunday and a peaceful village and cut out the run from the boundary when bowling.

This he did and bowled a medium paced ball which came off the bat and was well caught. On appeal, the Reverend gentleman shook his head firmly. The next ball, after a distinct click as it passed the bat, was caught by the wicket keeper. Everybody looked at the Vicar. 'I didn't hear anything,' said that worthy. This was too much for Larwood, who, casting instructions to the winds took his usual run from near the boundary and delivered a ball which the batsman didn't even see, but which removed his middle and off stump completely.

'Damn near miss that,' said Larwood as he walked back past the umpire.

But, to return to Littlehampton; what else is there to say before we move on up the coast. It was formerly an important ship building centre for vessels up to nine hundred tons. The bar, I always feel, is no bad thing as without it this attractive little harbour would long ago have become quite impossibly packed out. Unless you are lucky with your berth you may have to take the ground at low water, but you will be on soft mud and should stay reasonably upright. And don't forget to explore the river. The lower reaches are dominated by the great Norman keep of Arundel Castle, and above that the upper part runs through quite unspoilt country from one delightful little village to the next. Even Arundel is an attractive town, with picturesque houses running up its wide, steep street, while the villages beyond have each their little gem of a church with Saxon as well as Norman corners. There is good eating too and drinking in the Sussex pubs, so one way or the other, you should be able to do yourself proud.

A Nautical Interlude at Little Burpham

And don't, please, go away with the impression of Sussex you might get if you only visited Brighton and Hove. There are a lot of funny things still happening not more than a bat's flight round the second turning left. Only last week a retired N.O. friend of mine told me an odd story over beer and sandwiches in the local. We had been talking of the old days and I made a silly remark that the twentieth century was getting a bit humdrum. He gave me an odd look and said:

'Well, I wouldn't exactly say that — if you lived in our own village of Little Burpham, seven miles up the Arun from Little-hampton Harbour. Do you remember the great gale we had at the end of March last year after a suspiciously mild winter?' my friend said. 'Well the village won't forget it for some time because that night the elements fairly gave us all they had been storing up for weeks. There was a terrific gale of wind accompanied by lightning and an especially loud clap of thunder about three o'clock in the morning. Indeed, the 0630 shipping forecast talked of Force ten gales in the channel gusting even above that.

So, of course, I dressed a bit early and went out to see what damage had been done, because it was a sou'wester and our valley acts as a sort of wind tunnel when there is a gale from this direction, the steep sides constrict the air and increase the power and pressure of the wind in some odd way. Well there were a few hen houses where they shouldn't have been and tiles and chimney pots in the street and one great elm that had been blown down opposite the post office but as far as I could see, no really major damage had been done. I mean, little Miss Medhurst's Moonrise Cot was still firmly on the village green and the corrugated iron roof of the new village hall still tortured the morning air like a plastic passion flower. Dan Wigan in the yard of the *Cross Keys*, our one local, was looking faintly puzzled and I stopped to ask what was eating him.

"Well, I don't rightly know," he said, "I can't make it out. There's something I don't understand in the broccoli field."

I might explain that, like most country pubs, Dan had a small farm attached to the *Cross Keys*. After a pause he said,

"It looks like a boat of sorts. It can't be the cricket pavilion come over the hedge because it's got a sort of mast."

"Nonsense, Dan," I said, "It's too early in the morning to be seeing boats in Little Burpham!"

But I could tell he was worried so I said,

"Well, anyway, let's go down and have a look at it."

And we walked round the bar through the coppice wood at the back, along the valley slope and got to the gate of Dan's field. It was a small field with high earth hedges and there was no doubt about it — cosily tucked in between the banks and nestling on the spring cabbages as if it were in dry dock ready for repairs was a certain something.....a boat of sorts.

But it was a queer shaped vessel with two very broad square ends surmounted by carved red painted bannisters and a thick double stayed mast with a great iron lantern dangling from the hounds. Dan looked at it with a sort of Biblical resignation,

"D'ye think if we go back and have breakfast it will go away? I mean Annie was countin' on the broccoli an' cabbages for the young farmers' annual dinner dance. She 'ont like it one little bit!"

"No," I said, "It looks a bit too solid to go away on its own accord and there's nothing dreamlike about it except the shape. I mean if we weren't in England and a full seven miles up from the sea I'd say it was a Chinese junk. We'd best go and check it over I think."

There was certainly nothing in the least other worldly about its solid tarred clinker built top sides, which were rough and cold and wet to the touch. The thing that puzzled me was that the spring cabbages didn't seem to have sustained much damage from the storm tossed weight that had landed on them and I estimated the hull must weigh all of 150 tons if an ounce.

We were just wondering what to do next — I mean neither Dan nor I knew whether to ring up the Littlehampton Harbour Master or the Pulborough Municipal Disposals Department, or whether to fetch George Summers the village policeman and let him cope — you see, we'd never had a boat in Little Burpham before; added to which I had a sneaking suspicion that the necessary explanation was bound to sound a little bizarre over the telephone at 10 a.m. on a spring morning. But our attention was caught, at that moment, by the appearance on deck of a short, round and very smiling little man who I took to be the skipper — with features faintly reminiscent of a certain hospitable oriental gentleman much in the news at the moment. He was still dressed in wet oilskins as if he had not long finished snugging down and was now looking forward to a well earned breakfast, perhaps the first he had had in port for some days. He gave us 'good day' with just that faint oriental drawl over the vowels that so often makes English acquired by cultured foreigners so attractive — especially continental women. Having ventured the hope that the peace of the morning might rest lightly upon us he introduced himself as Captain Tee Wang, and seeing us eyeing the Chinese writing on the bulwarks with some interest he explained,

"In you honoured but veree funnee language eet would say, *Moon of Many Tomorrows*, but now, you come to my sheep, so you are obviously in want of something from me. Tell me what, so I can give wings to your charming desires." And the skipper bowed his smiles and looked expectantly at me. I looked at Daniel and back and even felt the rough hull again to reassure myself. Dan fidgeted and said,

Arundel Castle from the River

"Well, it's like this, you see, we don't want to seem inhospitable but this *is* my wife's favourite cabbage patch – an'.....an' she won't be best please," he finished lamely. The skipper looked suddenly concerned.

"But, my most English of comrades, I am destroyed with fraternal remorse if I am in wrong place – sometimes wandering paths of navigation can be straightened by the bulldozer of truth. Last night I take star fix and get what you say 'cooked hat' over sea, then clouds come and I get nuddings but liddle beacons. Haf I not indeed landed in the harbour of restful waters – how you call eet on zee chart of Admiraltee – Little Hompton? Our chairman he tell us of thee new hospitalitee in your Eengland. Zo, I call in passing, is it not deleecious?"

I explained, in what I hoped was an understanding tone of voice, that though he might have made his landfall at Littlehampton he was now well beyond it up the Arun Valley. The little man spread his hands out in a gesture of pure wonderment.

"Zo, I must have carried leetle too much way – no? I go further up harbour than I intend! Bot, I think it is understandable. There were many liddle wild horses in zee vint last night – did you not hear him?"

Dan nodded and as there seemed to be a bit of a lull developing in the conversation, from the expectant look on our friend's face, I said,

"How long had you planned to stay?"

"Oh, a veek or so at most, vile I recruit one or two new crew to replace a so regrettable liddle accident. I mean, while I enjoy your so deleecious personal company, I am unfortunately also run out of some vital things for the cooking, like soya sauce an' bamboo shoots and water chestnuts perhaps and Fragrant Petal says to get some ink fish and brushed prawns for her Chow Mein and crispy noodles. Plis to say to me, vere do I get zem?"

Dan said he had better come back to the *Cross Keys* where we could sort things out in comfort and perhaps talk to his wife but the skipper clasped his hands together and shook his head vigorously at the suggestion.

"Zat is delicious suggestion but eet is not permitted in zee rules of zee voyage and our Chairman Mao, who is so guideful with hees penetrating thoughts, is not allowing eet unless disqualifications, you see. I am rounding zee vorld in my leetle sheep, as Chairman has heard that rounding zee vorld is goot for international face – you know like peeng pong an' United Nations an' treeky Deexon."

"But," I said without thinking, "Haven't you heard? It's already been done – both ways as a matter of fact."

The smile broadened and in the tone of voice one uses to a rather dim child he said,

"But you see, I do eet backvords. Zat is zee secret weapon off China – zee junk. Only a Chinees Junk can go both vays. Eff I go op zee wrong sea, I seemply turn sail back to front and I go backvorts — I have rudder op both ends — see? But I am not allowed to set my foot upon the land until I have got to home port again in Canton — ven I have rounded the whole vorld. But zere ees nooding to say *you* cannot come aboard the *Moon of Many Tomorrows* which would be quite delicious and we will drink rice spirits and it will bring happiness to you both from zee inside. Later perhaps you can fetch me a few things and a new sheepmate or so from your so experienced Leetlehampton sailors."

Dan looked hestitant but I gave him an encouraging smile because, I don't mind admitting it, it is always rather fun looking round other people's boats. So, we clambered up the rather thin rope ladder aboard. Inside, the cabin was very snug with red carpets and gaily coloured curtains, patterned with roses and a collection of Chinese and Indian carved ornaments, together with old fashioned polished brass lamps in gimbals. An enchanting little poppet brought in the wine, dressed, not in the now familiar blue dungarees of her countrywomen, but in a long flowered gown caught in at the waist and rather reminiscent of an off beat Victorian tea gown. We were solemnly introduced to Fragrant Petal.

After the fourth glass and a lot of interesting talk, Daniel was getting expansive and pregnant with ideas about bamboo shoots and things. In fact he told the skipper that there was a Chinese restaurant in Pulborough and he would send the odd job boy in to bring provisions as long as he had a clear written list and was hinting at money in advance. I left them to it and had time to gaze idly out of the portholes which were as large as most cottage windows. It was an odd sensation I found, to be looking down at the fishes swimming lazily in and out of the broccoli and now and then having a passing nibble at the new spring cabbage shoots.

Eventually we went home — I always find going down ladders more difficult even when there is not much of a sea but as Dan said, sitting about in a Chinese junk all day wouldn't get the baby a new shirt and we'd better get weaving with the day's chores. In fact I was so busy all day, what with the garden being behindhand and a visit from Miss Pogson who is secretary of the local amenity society and rather terrifying, that I almost forgot about our visiting yachtsmen until I went to see Mrs Westcott, the postmistress, for the evening mail. And there was a large parcel off the bus labelled,

Captain Tee Wang,
Moon of Many Tomorrows
C/o Little Burpham Post Office — to be called for.
Just then in came Daniel's boy and told me he had been down and
written out a list of provisions and telephoned them to Pulborough in
time for the evening bus.

When we took them down there was quite a crowd and the boy
was worried about damage to Mrs Dan's cabbages. But we cleared a
path and a temporary signpost was put up to warn folk to keep to it.

After that, the village seemed to accept Captain Wang for the
time being; I gather a sprinkling of the village lads went down more
often than they admitted, just to 'chat up' Fragrant Petal on the
quiet, but no harm seemed to be done. Even complaints from certain
parents about their young returning home a little the worse for drink
were felt to be slightly stuffy in this day and age, even in the wilds
of Sussex.

But it was not until Saturday, when as most people know, we
celebrate the birth of our local and rather unusual Saint Gilbert with
a bit of a spring fête, that the captain really came into his own. The
village ladies, inspired by Fragrant Petal, rather than the Vicar, surprised a delighted village, and indeed themselves, by giving birth to
some most unusual, if oriental flower arrangements. But it was the
gallant Captain who really made our day by producing Chinese fire
crackers which he let off with great abandon and an entire disregard
for safety regulations from the foredeck. All would have been well if
the Vicar hadn't been moved to try his hand. Having little sense of
direction at the best of times, it was a pity he chose a colourful and
very powerful rocket — a planet-buster, I think it was called. Anyway
he despatched it, after one false start, straight up King Alfred's Lane
into poor old Major Wilfred's herbarium — where it burst into a
splendid constellation of red stars and a noble shattering of plate
glass. Oh well, I expect it will all be the same forty years hence —
though to give everybody their due, there was surprisingly little
damage done, barring a few tiles cracked and by next morning a self
appointed fatigue squad had cleaned up *Moon of Many Tomorrows*
and swabbed the foredeck down. Unfortunately I had to go to town
for a few days and when I returned I looked automatically over the
trees for the mast — yes, it was still there, so I strolled down to the
broccoli field to pass the time of day with my friend Wang — reflect-
ing that he himself seemed to have become everybody's friend by

now. It was a fearsome looking sky with a hard black squall line building up in the west. Inside, the lamps were lit and I saw young Jones the bank and his 'steady', Mavis of Pine Tree Cottage, helping Fragrant Petal to finish some ornamental rope work.

I gave the gallant captain 'good e'en' and he wished me a smooth passage through the month of Cherry Blossom.

"Tonight," he said with the look of distant horizons in his eyes, "It is in the stars that I leave you — with great sadnesses but also many memories of your harbour of a thousand enchantments. May my extreme felicitations cushion your footfalls into the to-morrow."

I was taken completely aback I'm afraid, having almost for-gotten what the captain had originally said about the temporary nature of his visit. I mean, he was already so much a natural part of the community — and in the village we dislike change.

"But you can't go tonight," I said, "Just look at the sky — haven't you heard the weather forecast?"

He smiled reassuringly.

"No," he replied, "A thousand blessings upon your....how you call it, Met; we are not quite on same wavelength but we have our own Chairman's so splendid book. It is more consistent we find. Anyway, time is come that I go — I know it through my inside. Truly is it written 'Destiny has four feet, eight hands and sixteen eyes. I shall go, about the third gong stroke of the night. And now my dear, dear friend, I say to you a full day and a gentle passing into night when the time is come. Do not look for me again — but I theenk of you when I am far away, at the back of the wind."

Well, I'm afraid I always find 'good byes' a little embarrassing, so I wished him a fair wind and a quick passage and just then the first large drops of rain began to fall and I remembered I had on my one and only 'city slicker' suit so I shot off back home to change and have a quick drink before the storm really opened up. It turned out to be one of those nights when dark comes very suddenly and indeed the great line of black squall clouds seemed to sweep across and envelope the whole valley, in one onrush. Before we knew where we were, we were into the second great storm of the season of equinoxial gales. There was no going out in this tearing wind and horizontally driving rain, so after supper we played a little bridge and went to bed. Fork lightning began to play during the night and I think it was about three o'clock that it happened.

There was a louder and longer crack and then an uneasy silence, as if the eye of the storm had just reached the village and was poised momentarily above it. I got up to look out and there, just above the tree tops against the inky black sky I could see the loom of a ship with all sails set. The navigation lights were on and the portholes ablaze. High up, the masthead light moved like a strange star across the storm clouds as the ship passed seawards, into the empty blackness of the night — backwards. Then there was a crack of wind and the whole silence splintered into movement and noise. I drew the curtains and got thoughtfully back into bed.

Next morning, as I was shaving I had a sudden thought — when I left the night before, young Jones and his Mavis had been still aboard! I dressed a bit sharpish like and as the rain had stopped and there was a distinct easing of the wind, I went down with Dan to the cabbage field beyond the wood. It was no use pretending to myself — I knew it would be empty and it was. I noticed one odd thing in spite of my preoccupation, the crops didn't appear to have suffered much damage. I mentioned my worry about the young folk to Dan and he said he would ask their parents about them. When I looked in later in the evening there had been a certain amount of speculation in the *Cross Keys* about Mr Wang's rather hurried departure, but in Sussex we take things much as they come I'm afraid, without asking too many questions.

That would have been about all — except for two very odd things. Nobody in Little Burpham has seen or heard from Mavis or the Jones boy since. The parents admitted rather reluctantly that they had threatened to run away and get married on more than one occasion and now they supposed it had happened — probably in Scotland. I personally doubted very much whether, if there had indeed been any wedding it had been in Scotland; but I came to the conclusion that it was really no business of mine how Chinese skippers acquired their crew. I am sure they would have written at least, if they had wanted anything.

The other queer thing was that Annie's Young Farmers' Dinner was a roaring success, especially the broccoli and spring cabbage — which were both said to taste so deliciously unlike any other cabbage that had ever been raised in the village. In fact, funnily enough, it was agreed that they tasted just as if they had been well soused in what the village had got used to calling 'spirits of rice' — it makes you wonder!'

Well, Sussex is like that, I said as we got up to go home.

Shoreham

I have a sneaking suspicion that you will probably want to skip this next harbour along the coast. Its power station and gasworks are useful as a landmark, for there is nothing else quite like them among the holiday resorts of this Sussex coast and if you were in real trouble you would be grateful to know that you can get in here at any state of the tide. But, under normal conditions it is no place for yachtsmen. It is a busy commercial harbour where the only possible place for yachts is through the lock in the Eastern Arm and into the canal, but even here the casual arrival will not be welcome and all the books advise you to make arrangements in advance. To me, this immediately spoils the joy of cruising – the freedom to go where you want when you want, without having to make detailed plans in advance. Long ago it was a Celtic entry port and then, as now, a man might run a little sailing ship across to Dieppe between the hours of sunrise and sunset on a summer's day – perhaps the happiest thought with which to leave Shoreham.

Newhaven

So we sail east, past the impressive white piles on Brighton's water front. I cannot help remembering when passing this place that Defoe found it 'a poor fishing town', adding,

> 'The sea is very unkind to this town, and has by its
> continual encroachments, so gain'd upon them, that
> in a little time more they might reasonably expect
> it would eat up the whole town.'

Wishful thinking maybe – but it's still there I'm afraid. The next port, Newhaven, is really the only fully satisfactory port of refuge on this part of the South coast, so most of us find ourselves in there from time to time. The town itself has little to commend it and even the shops, good as they are, lie some distance from the harbour. In fact, as its name implies, it really is a new harbour. It used to be known as the village of Meeching when the Ouse came out a few miles to the east at Seaford. But in 1570 there was a great storm and the river found a much easier way to the sea, forming in the process, a safe and comfortable harbour. If you are feeling poor you can go

on down the harbour to the Harbour Master's office and he will find
you a berth tied up to the staging or to another boat. For comfort,
however, I would advise you to go into the Cresta Marine Yacht
Harbour in Sleepers Hole. I can assure those that know the Friesian
Islands, it is quite unlike the watershed, also called *slapersbucht*
(Sleepers Hole) in the *Riddle of the Sands* country between Delfzyl

Godwits

and Nordeney. I remember we once played bridge there while waiting
for water, with half a gale sweeping across the desolate waste of sea
and sand and torrential rain drumming on the cabin roof.

Here at Newhaven it was a friendly welcome from the Marina
harbour master, and help in tying up; then a walk round the pontoons to find out if any friends had come. They had, and we all had
an excellent dinner at the *Sheffield Arms*. We enjoyed ourselves so
much that we all decided to stay another day. Incidentally, if like us
you arrive there after the shops are shut on a Saturday night you will
be interested to know that the Post Office in Gibbon Road, more or
less opposite the entrance to the Yacht Harbour is open till noon on

Sundays and keeps a good range of food.

If indeed you do get gale bound, don't forget there is some jolly attractive country just inland. There is Blackcap Down with its tuft of pines and saddle of beeches where poor old Simon De Montfort's men charged down on the waiting King's men in those hopeful days before oblivion. And across the Lewes Gap to the east, lies a wonderful amphitheatre of hills beloved of Gilbert White on his way to Ringmer. Here are secret lanes, white with cow parsley and pink with the wild campion and with great blue patches of milkwort and yellow vetches. Between the hills lie enchanted villages of the old Belgic tribes long since driven underground by the land hungry Saxon barbarians — villages like Caburn (Caer Bryon — the city on the hill) on whose grassy slopes was built the last great ramparted, fortified hill town of Celtic Sussex.

Even back on the sea beaches you will find the cheerful stonecrop shining in the sun and lady's slipper and sea poppies. On the way back from a walk last time, I fell in with the coastguard and in the course of swapping yarns as one does, he told me a few of the local problems of the Lifeboat men. Typical of these was the urgent call three weeks before, to go to the help of a motor boat fishing some way offshore. When the lifeboat got there they were asked to take the children off — not because of any breakdown but because Grannie had been promised they would be home by 4.30 p.m. In answer to the coxswain's, 'Why the hell can't *you* take them in' — the bland answer was 'We haven't finished fishing yet!'

Truly they come in all shapes and sizes and perhaps I had better not say what I would have done with them.

Lastly, if you like the informal atmosphere of Glyndbourne — don't forget it is only a few miles up country to the east of Lewes.

The Downs

There is one little suggestion for anyone leaving Newhaven and in a hurry to reach the East Coast. If you leave about an hour before the east going tidal stream and can keep up an average speed of about five knots you will find that you can keep the tide for a whole twelve hours. As you go east it gets later and later along the coast, and just when you would lose the flood tide off Dover you catch the ebb up the coast to Ramsgate, some twelve miles further on.

Going east from Newhaven the next little hole in the coast worth investigating is of course Rye, some thirty miles away and here your E.T.A. will depend firmly on the state of the tide. There is no navigation, not even any pilotage on this rather dull passage, so while we are still in sight of the Downs we may be forgiven a few last thoughts.

In the early days, these chalk downs with their light soil and sparse vegetation were the only areas that primitive man, with his inadequate tools could cultivate, so we find his remains all over the place and — in case you have forgotten — as late as about seven thousand years ago he didn't need a boat to get there. He just walked over from the continent when he felt like it, because there was no Channel! England was still joined to the mainland from about the middle of the North Sea, where the Rhine and the Thames flowed out together, to somewhere round about Beachy Head or even further west. When the sea broke through, some time in the fifth or sixth millennium B.C. it was at first very narrow and consequently tides were really vicious and little skin boats had to wait for slack tide before it was possible to get across. That was why the Iberian Megalithic people from the Mediterranean funked it and sailed up the Irish Sea to land in Wales and the Bristol Channel. Later, when the Channel had grown to something like its present width, the short crossing was still popular with the invaders and the stretch of shore from Dover to Beachy Head far more welcoming and with better and easier natural harbours than it has today.

But a lot of the simple things that gave pleasure to early man are still there for us to enjoy. There are the quiet villages in the corners of the hills and the ever changing woods, breezy grassland and the downland flowers, especially the harebell, clustered bell-flower, the birdsfoot trefoil and the horseshoe and kidney vetches; wild orchids, including the rare ones like the fragrant, the bee, the blunt tipped and the early spider; and best of all the spiked rampion which only grows in one corner of East Sussex. Nor would these be complete without the Downland birds — the larks rising in succession and the linnets singing in patches of gorse and juniper, while now and then if you are lucky you hear the corn bunting and the rare Dartford warbler and see his prey, the burnet moth and small blue butterfly. The famous Southdown sheep were developed here in the eighteenth century and, helped by hares and rabbits, kept the grass short enough for the flowers to flourish.

I doubt if the better looking girls among the sheep would be flattered by Arthur Young's description:—

> 'The shoulders are wide; they are round and straight in the barrel; broad upon the loin and hips; shut well in the twist, which is a projection of flesh in the inner part of the thigh that gives a fulness when viewed behind, and makes a South Down leg of mutton remarkably round and short, more so than in most other breeds.!
>
> 'The South Down farmers breed their sheep with faces and legs of a colour, just as suits their fancy. One likes black, another sandy, a third speckled, and one and all exclaim against white.'

Now this is all being threatened by powerful tractors ploughing it all up to create a prairie for barley. One can only hope that a little will be preserved in its original form so that wandering man may continue to refresh his soul in relative peace.

The Cinque Ports

We have had the South Downs as a background ever since we left Chichester harbour, but here at Beachy Head they come to an end with a grand flourish and give way to a strange area of flat marshy shores as far as Folkestone, broken only by an obtruding ridge of The Weald which comes down to the coast at Hastings. It is an area where you would expect to find a continual battle to prevent encroachments from the sea and along part of the coast this is so, yet elsewhere, surprisingly it is the land which has won the battle. Forts which were once on the coast stand in the middle of nowhere and old harbours are left high and dry two or three miles inland.

The military, political and economic importance of this part of the coast facing the Continent at the narrowest part of the Channel, will be obvious. The defender would want to fortify it to keep his enemies out and the invader would be just as interested in preserving these fortifications, once captured, to give him a strong and defensible bridgehead. So, right round the coast from Beachy Head to the Thames you can crack your shins on buildings which would warm the cockles of the most sluggish Local Historical Society. Signs of Celtic occupation give way to Roman ruins and corners of Saxon buildings are embedded in the great Norman forts and churches which bristle at every corner.

Most are connected in some way with the naval defences, such as they were, because no English King before the seventeenth century could afford a Navy — at best they owned a few ships to be supplemented in time of need by impressing shipping from nearby ports. This right of course had to be paid for by the grant of privileges and immunities and this was how the confederacy of the Cinque Ports

Seven Sisters from Seaford Head.   (Photo Ben Darby).

Looking across Ramsgate Harbour towards the Goodwins.

Margate - Quite an important harbour in the days of the Thames' Ferries.

A corner of old Whitstable.

came into existence, probably in Saxon times. Its members enjoyed something approaching a monopoly of cross Channel trade and communications. In return they had to supply the King with a fleet of fifty-seven ships for fifteen days each year, together with a master, twenty men and a boy.

The original members of the confederacy were Hastings, Romney, Hythe, Dover and Sandwich. They were joined later by Winchelsea and Rye and each port could, if it wished, acquire 'limbs' that is additional ports, which would enjoy a share of both privileges and obligations. In this way, ports like Seaford, Pevensey, Folkestone and Margate came to be associated with the organisation. The relative importance of the main ports in the thirteenth century can be gauged best by the allocation between them of the quota of fifty-seven ships. Dover, though not the earliest member of the Confederacy was already much the most important, contributing twenty-one ships. Winchelsea come next with ten, followed by Hastings with six and Hythe, Sandwich, Rye and Romney with five each. The post of 'Admiral of the Fleet of the Cinque Ports' seems to have been invented to reward somebody who had made himself useful about 1300. As you will remember the Barons of the Cinque Ports still have the honour of holding a canopy over the King's Head at Coronations while the office of Lord Warden has been held by a long succession of eminent men including Sir Winston Churchill.

One of the privileges granted to the Cinque Port towns was that of self-government with the somewhat curious stipulation that notice to elect a Mayor had to be given by a trumpeter at midnight. Freemen of these towns could use the title 'baron' and dress in white cotton jumper suits, with a red St George's Cross on the breast and back and the arms of the port underneath. They must have looked a treat for sore eyes as they travelled to market places throughout the Kingdom exercising their right of free tolls. The inhabitants were exempted from military service and in return had to take an oath of allegiance to the Ports and the Sovereign; any rash enough to refuse were promptly turned out of their houses and the house sealed up or pulled down. But they had a lot of fun on the way, Romney for instance spent a great deal of money producing the famous Romney Play which drew crowds from all round the neighbourhood while at both Romney and Hythe the corporations kept up the old custom of presenting 'porpuses' (porpoises) to the lord's table at Saltwood.

I can't help wondering what they would be up to today if their ports hadn't run out of water and ended up miles inland. As you know, of the original five, only Dover survives as a busy port, and Rye, which we will look in to next, of the later additons. As we pass, a word or two about the 'has beens'.

Pevensey

As every prep school historian knows, William the Conqueror stumbled ashore here and had to think quickly to laugh off an incident which his followers might have interpreted as an ill omen. I always think it is interesting to remember that if William hadn't been gale bound in St Valéry for a month, allowing time for the Danes to strike first in the North and get a bloody nose from a fresh Saxon army, thus lifting the watch on the Channel and decimating the defence troops, William might have been walloped and we would have become a Danish colony instead! I just wonder however, exactly where he landed, for in those days there was no nice, gently shelving beach at Pevensey up which the invaders could run their boats. There was just a group of tiny islands near the shore on one of which stood a famous castle, the *Anderida* of the Romans which in some form still existed to be raided by Earl Godwin in 1042 and 1049. This was far too good a site to waste and William gave it to Robert, Count of Mortain, who built the massive Keep which stands out so boldly from the sea, even if today if rises from the middle of a flat plain. Of its numerous seiges during the next four hundred years this is not the place to write and by the time of the Armada it was obviously so derelict that it was ordered to be either rebuilt or destroyed. Nothing seems to have been done, but its usefulness as a castle was over. As late as 1700 Pevensey was still at least a small local fishing port. Then it began to silt up. The Castle is now a mile inland and the rather unattractive bit of shingle beach is known as the Crumbles. This bit of coast remained both vulnerable and important and it is here that in the Napoleonic Wars the line of Martello towers, which stretch right up the East Coast starts.

Hastings

In its heyday as the leading Cinque Port, Hastings had a good natural harbour and its importance was enhanced by the cliffs which provided a commanding site for its fort. Its name comes from Haesten, the Jute, who landed here about 400 A.D. but this was late in the

town's history when you think of the neolithic remains which have
been found on East Hill. Then the sea swallowed up much of the old
town, two harbours and the Priory. Today there is no pretence at a
harbour and the fishermen and yachts are pulled up on the beach.

Winchelsea

Winchelsea next door is even more unlucky for it is no longer on
the sea at all, being three miles inland. Standing on an island, it was a
Saxon port, a shipbuilding centre and, in the thirteenth century, a royal
dockyard. Then in October 1250 there was a terrible night recorded
dramatically by some unknown writer:—

'The moon, upon her change, appearing exceeding red
and swelled, began to show tokens of the great
tempest of wind that followed, which was so huge
and mightie, both by land and sea, that the like had
not been lightlie knowne, and seldome, or rather
never, heard of by men then alive. The sea forced
contrarie to his natural course, flowed twice without
ebbing, yeelding such a rooring that the same was
heard (not without great wonder) a farre distance in
from the shore.'

But, though this storm destroyed most of the ships, several churches
and about three hundred houses, the town was not yet finished. It
survived to be sacked by the French a few years later and it took a
second storm in February 1287 before the town was 'drowned'. With
royal support a new, walled town was built on a safer site, but Winchelsea was still intended to be a port and was prosperous enough in the
next century to be worth further attention by the French. It was,
however, the sea which was to have the last word. Foiled in its attempt
to drown the town it decided instead to leave it to its own devices and
gently receded. By 1450 one of the Cinque Ports had already gone —
inland.

Rye

The one port left along this stretch of coast is a bit, funny
peculiar, as they say, but fun if you can spare the time. One look at the
chart will remind you that it has only survived by the skin of its teeth,

for the entrance dries out for about three cables and the town itself is a
good mile from the harbour. The harbour is really a separate little
village with its own church, post office and shop, chandlery, slip and
two pubs — the *Inkerman Arms* and the *William the Conqueror*, right
on the quay, which offers hot snacks. You can stay down in there and
get the harbour master to find you a berth against the catwalk but I
think it is even more fun to go up to the town and berth against Strand

The town quay, Rye.

Quay taking the ground in soft mud. Incidentally, if you don't like
taking the mud, don't come into Rye except possibly at neaps. Even
then you will be lucky to find a berth where you can stay afloat.

But, you know, the old town really is a dream with its cobbled
streets and old timbered houses with their projecting gables. Tied up at
the Strand Quay, or wandering round to the fish market, you will never
be nearer to seeing a Cinque Port as it must have been in the great days
of its past glories. Here the ships would come to load up with their

cargo of good English wool while the merchants drank their ale in *The Mermaid* in the intervals of waiting the return of their other ships with cargoes of wine or silks. If you are interested in old clocks you should make a point of going into the church; the clock is said to be the oldest in England, dated 1560 and still going strong. The church is well worth a visit for its own sake but then so are the old streets and the Landgate and the twelfth century Ypres Tower and the *George Inn* with its musicians' gallery not to mention *The Ship* and the *Old Bell*. In any case you will have no excuse for not doing so, unless you can find a lot to do aboard, because having come in with the tide you won't be able to get out again for another twelve hours!

Romney Marsh

Dungeness was never an attractive headland, however lyrical the naturalists get and the nuclear power station doesn't add to its attractions but it is at least a fine landmark and quite unmistakable if it looms out of that mist that has hidden the shore for the last two or three hours. Boats anchor on either side of the headland according to the wind, though it would not be my choice for a quiet night. Indeed, you can have a witch thrown in for good measure, if you read your Ingoldsby Legends, who

'May still be occasionally discovered in favourable,
i.e., stormy, seasons, weathering Dungeness Point in
an egg-shell, or careering on her broomstick over
Dymchurch wall.'

So watch it!

Romney of course is another of the Cinque Ports which has lost its harbour, but as we sail past I think we might be more interested in the strange world of Romney Marsh. First enclosed by the Romans, it has remained a queer sort of no man's land — as the Marsh folk say,

'the world's divided like into Europe, Ashy, Afriky,
Ameriky, Australy, an' Romney Marsh.'

Be that as it may, it was certainly an area which felt itself outside and perhaps above the law and where anyone who wanted to hide could find comparative safety. I always like Kipling's description of it in Puck of Pook's Hill:—

'The Marsh is just about riddled with diks an' sluices,
an' tide-gates an' water-lets. You can hear 'en bubb-
lin' an' grummelin' when the tide works in 'em, an'
then you hear the sea rangin' left and right-handed all
up along the Wall.'

You will remember that it was here that the fairies collected when they wanted to leave England, sending Puck to wake up Widow Whitgift and get her to lend her boat, with her two sons, one dumb and the other blind, as crew to sail them across to France. The fairies were just one more group who sought refuge in the Marsh. The place was generally stiff with medieval peasants who had run away from their lords, law-breakers, escaped prisoners of war, Royalists and Jacobites and of course pirates and smugglers.

Now, as I said in *East Anglia from the Sea*, I have kept off smuggling for most of our potter round the coast. Indeed I have got a little tired of reading about it, for I think there is hardly a seaside village anywhere round the South coast whose garrulous old men are not pregnant with stories of their local celebrities — at a pint a time. Anyway, you needn't go further than Kipling's delightful poem for the feel of this era of sea-going life:

'If you wake at midnight, and hear a horse's feet,
Don't go drawing back the blind, or looking in the street,
Them that asks no questions isn't told a lie.
Watch the wall, my darling, while the Gentlemen go by!
       Five and twenty ponies,
       Trotting through the dark —
       Brandy for the Parson,
       'Baccy for the Clerk;
       Laces for a lady; letters for a spy,
And watch the wall, my darling, while the Gentlemen go by!'

It was not only the local squires, justices and parsons who were in the game, the excisemen themselves could usually be bribed and even the Government — canny old businessmen — were busy during the Napoleonic wars smuggling British made boots for the French army through their own blockade. So no wonder ordinary smugglers provided an important part of the espionage service of both countries. Many of them were probably double agents and told the French about English shipping and defences just as readily as they collected French information to take back to England.

The delightful narrow gauge Romney, Hythe and Dymchurch railway is still running I think and even this little railway did its war service, dressed up with armour plating to provide transport along the edge of the Marsh. Hythe at the far end is another old port which is firmly ashore, and Folkestone, though flourishing enough, does not encourage visiting yachtsmen, except in emergency because the harbour is too small and too busy to accommodate them.

Dover

I would need a large dose of rum and Guinness to wax lyrical about Dover — as a yacht harbour, I hasten to add. But sooner or later most of us can't avoid using it, so we had better give it a little room in the sun. I don't think I need stress how busy the harbour is nowadays, and I cannot emphasise too strongly that this is one place where traffic control signals mean what they say. We yachtsmen are inclined to get a little casual about such signals because in so many harbours the authorities do not bother to show them for small boats unless they are in imminent danger of being mowed down by some monster. Here in Dover, however, *nobody* may go in and out without a signal. If you have to wait outside on anything but a calm day, you have my sympathy because it is one of the most uncomfortable bits of water I know. We had to do it once when we were going in before breakfast with a very seasick crew and by the end of half an hour Joan and I were also looking a bit green. When the entry signals at last went up for a cross Channel steamer we got firmly on his tail so that we could get through before the harbour master had time to change them again!

After waiting to get in you may be disappointed to find how difficult it is to find a peaceful and comfortable berth. The moorings and anchorage off the Prince of Wales Pier suffer from the swell which seems to come in most of the time and the Wellington Dock is open for only about one and a half hours before high water. Once inside it is comfortable enough, we have found but opinions seem to differ widely and violently on this score. It is reputed to be dirty with coal dust and so congested nowadays that it is advisable to phone in advance to find out whether there will be space.

I can't help thinking of rats, not because they are more addicted to Dover than elsewhere but because it was a famous judge's wife from these parts, when told that the only really satisfactory way to clear them out of her house was to stop up their holes, made the immortal remark at an official banquet, 'But aren't they rather difficult to catch?'

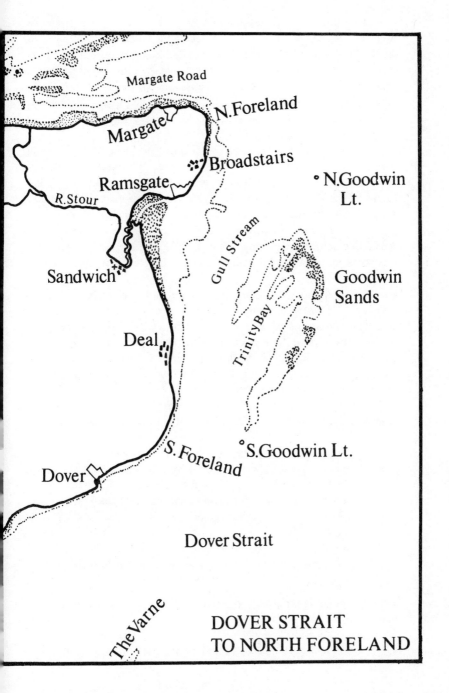

DOVER STRAIT
TO NORTH FORELAND

Dover itself is a pleasant enough town with a very attractive Regency terrace, Waterloo Crescent, facing the harbour. I don't need to say that it is stuffed with history, not to mention the castle stuck up on the hill, but I must just mention the lighthouse at the end of St Mary's Church in the Castle precincts, because this claims to be the oldest building in the British Isles, and really was built by the Romans to guide their ships across the Channel in the days when there was no compass to give them direction.

As the shortest way across the Channel, the Dover-Calais crossing has always been popular and by the seventeenth century a contemporary guide book claimed that it took only three hours. This was in one of the packet-boats, ships of about sixty tons with a single deck and cabins in the high stern which carried mail and passengers. Whatever the guide book claimed, three hours sounds a bit optimistic and I would think only achieved with one hell of a wind up their tail! Four or five was more normal and this could easily extend to two or three days if things went wrong. In a calm, it was not unknown for rowing boats to go out in mid Channel to pick up passengers who might be in a hurry. Congreve completed the journey in this way once, the French oarsmen taking five hours to get him ashore — but even so, he arrived a good twelve hours before the Packet on which he set out. To the dangers of the sea were added the dangers from privateers, dangers so real that most travellers were advised to set off in their oldest clothes and carrying the minimum of cash and valuables.

Despite all the difficulties, by the early eighteenth century the extent of the regular traffic from Dover was impressive. Defoe tells us that,

> 'The packets for France go off here, as also those for
> Nieuport, with the mails for Flanders, and all those
> ships which carry freights from New-York to Holland,
> and from Virginia to Holland, come generally hither,
> and unlade their goods, enter them with, and show
> them to the custom-house officers, pay the duties,
> and then enter them again by certificate, reload them,
> and draw back the duty by debenture, and so they go
> away for Holland.'

All this was going on at a time when according to the same busy little man the town had,

> 'An ill repair'd, dangerous, and good for little harbour
> and pier, very chargeable and little worth.'

The Downs Anchorage

There is quite a lot to keep you amused between Dover and Ramsgate. First the famous white cliffs of the South Foreland – a lovely sight on the rare days when you can see them all the way across the Channel, and to us East Coasters a sign that we are a day's sail from home. For some reason the tide is always in a state which suggests that the Ramsgate Channel would be quicker than The Gull so we can measure our progress by the familiar landmarks – the lovely St Margaret's Bay, the Dover Patrol Memorial, 'conspic.' and Walmer Castle the official residence of the Lord Warden of the Cinque Ports. By then we should have picked up the Deal Bank buoy and Deal itself is in sight and, as the shoreline disappears into Pegwell Bay, Ramsgate itself appears in the distance with ordinary luck – because for some reason we seem to engender a sudden fog whenever we use this bit of coast.

This part of the coast up to Pegwell Bay looks so uninteresting nowadays that it is difficult to believe that it saw three of the most important landings in our history. Julius Caesar probably landed somewhere between Deal and Thanet in 55 B.C., after failing to get a foothold near Dover. Five hundred years later those two characters who sound rather like a music hall turn, Hengist and Horsa are thought to have landed at Ebbsfleet and conquered Kent for the Jutes and later on, St Augustine came ashore at about the same spot, confronted Ethelbert across the Stour and persuaded him that he and his forty monks were good men and should be allowed to stay. You will be relieved to hear that because of his choice of Thanet as a landing place there are now no snakes on the island.

Of course, there is also poor old St Mildred who seems to have been given her title for lying, as the old chronicler put it, 'in a hot oven three hours together'. Her reward was to be made the Patron Saint of Thanet and have a bay on the North Kent coast named after

Heron.

her. That would seem to give this corner of Kent a bit of a flying start, but if you really want an 'historical' potter you must wait for the tide and find the buoyed channel across the sands of Pegwell Bay into the Stour. When you get up to Richborough you will have reached the Roman *Rutupiae* and the site of one of our most impressive collections of Roman ruins in the country. Above this, the river has a depth of about seven feet and you can go on and visit the last of our Cinque Ports, Sandwich, which like Rye, is a fascinating old town. The Barbican should remind you that Henry VIII was a bit worried about this corner of his Kingdom and built a chain of block houses through Walmer and Deal. But this coast was already silting up and when a large ship owned by the Pope was careless enough to sink in the fairway this was the end for it acted like a magnet and rapidly collected enough sand and mud round it to block the rest of the channel.

One forgets that all these early invaders like the Romans and Saxons didn't have to sail round the North Foreland, where there always seems to be a unpleasant little chop, to reach the Thames, because Thanet was still an island and they could use the shorter, safer route between it and the mainland of Kent and up the Wantsum to Reculver. Bede tells us that this river was about three furlongs broad and was only fordable in two places. It probably remained navigable until about the end of the fifteenth century. Since then Thanet has only once reverted to an island and that was in the bad floods of 1953.

Ramsgate

You will find the Pier Master just as meticulous as at Dover about the use of traffic signals. I know no other port where these go up so promptly as they do at Ramsgate — that is once they are certain that you really want to go in. It is just as well, for the tide can run fast round the Quern and beating back may be a slow job. Opinions differ about Ramsgate as a port, but we ourselves are very fond of it. It is true that the outer harbour is uncomfortable except on the rare occasions when there is a dead calm, and if you do not want to be up all night fending off and tending warps you will have to lock in to the inner harbour which is only open for about two hours near H.W. This limits your starting time the next day and is particularly tiresome if you are going south as you get out just about the time the tide starts to turn in the wrong direction. If, however, you want a day or two to rest and recover, to replenish the stores and look after your boat, then you could find no more comfortable place than the inner harbour at Ramsgate. There is one drawback — it's rather like being at a zoo — but on the wrong side of the wire. Like the Mappin Terraces, the pontoons are just under the main road and promenade — and the supply of little boys, stones and garbage seems inexhaustible. Bored East End Matrons bring their reluctant broods to see the funny men in their little boats. The Dockmaster may find you a berth, if someone is away, otherwise you tie up on the quay to starboard. There are really helpful boatyards if you need them and a friendly and hospitable club, the *Royal Temple* up on the cliff with a magnificent view over the harbour. It used to be exciting having a shower in the basement when there was no certainty which end of the machine the water would come out, but last time we called in and signed the book, all was well and, most important, the beer machine was working splendidly. Even if you are not paying a courtesy call you should walk up to somewhere near the club for the view over the harbour and the Goodwins.

On reflection, I don't seem to be able to dredge up from memory any fascinating bits of history about Ramsgate, no picturesque streets, buildings or ruins for you to go and see — so you are let off. It is just a good, bustling honest-to-God holiday resort. I'm afraid I haven't even discovered why people go there, as most of them look rather depressed as they wander round the town engrossed apparently in deciding which of twenty or so fish and chip shops they will patronise that day. We have found they are all good — at least on the number of occasions we have come up channel from the French coast and sent someone ashore to buy the quickest meal for a tired crew. It has invariably been excellent even after a journey back to *Kala Sona* in a newspaper. If you want something a little more exotic than fish and chips, I don't really think I can do better than point you at the Chinese Restaurant, five minutes from the harbour — anyone will tell you where — because the hotels don't automatically send one into transports of delighted anticipation.

Perhaps we have been unlucky when leaving Ramsgate, but it always seems to happen at about 0200 hours in sheeting rain and an uncomfortable wind that is unfortunately just not bad enough to form an excuse for remaining in port.

The Overland Route

As you go up the coast you should really drop your sails off Broadstairs, in salute — not, I hasten to add, to Mr Edward Heath, whatever your politics, nor to the memory of Queen Victoria who lived here as a child, but because there was here a Chapel of Our Lady of Bradstow that was so revered that conscientious sailors used to drop their sails in salute. The North Foreland light was built during the reign of Charles II and from here, when we are in a hurry to get home, we strike straight across the Thames Estuary, up one of the Edinburgh Channels, across the Black Deep to No. 9 Barrow and then by Swin No. 1, the SW Middle to the Whitaker Beacon. I would not of course try this in fog, but on a clear day it is a fascinating passage and when it is calm the buoys marking the different channels stand up like rows of street lamps.

On this cruise, however, we propose to take you along the Kent Coast and up the Medway; after which we will have a look at the south bank of the Thames, just as we did the north bank in the first book of this series — *East Anglia from the Sea*.

We could of course sail to the Medway as the big ships do, by the Queens or Princes Channels, but there is so much that is interesting along the North Kent coast that I suggest we take the inshore passage, known to most of us as the Overland Route. The tides are a bit dodgy round the North Foreland as they make from two directions and a favourable tide up coast may be adverse when you get round the corner. You will generally see a few ships tossing uneasily at anchor in the quarantine berth in the Margate Roads, and rolling about rather unexpectedly, because although you have entered the

Oare Creek - A typical mooring off the Swale.

Rochester Castle from the moorings.

The Thames' skyline still retains its magical quality.

London going to bed across the water.

Thames estuary here and are under the jurisdiction of the Port of London Authority it does not mean that you are going to find smooth water. Even the deepest channel is very shallow and the many banks produce all sorts of odd swirls and rough patches. I can't help remembering a passage in that enchanting book, the *Ingoldsby Legends,*

'When you've passed by the Nore, and you hear the winds roar
In a manner you scarce could have fancied before,
　　When the cordage and tackling are flapping and crackling,
　　And the boy with the bell thinks it useless to tell
You that's "dinner on table," because you're unwell;
　　When above you all's "scud," and below you the flood
Looks a horrible picture of soap-suds and mud,
　　When the timbers are straining, And folks are complaining,
The dead-lights are letting the spray and the rain in,
　　When the helm'sman looks blue, And Captain Large too,
And you really don't know what on earth you shall do.'

The Reculver Towers, a landmark for over six hundred years.

Margate

But I think we should move on west a few miles and look in at Margate. Its main function as a port nowadays is to cater for the holiday makers — and this incidentally does not include yachtsmen who are not at all welcome in the small drying out harbour. This is only a relatively recent development because, if you remember, transport by road and rail has only replaced water transport here for the last one hundred and fifty years. Up to then, with bad roads infested by highwaymen, the discomforts of a passage by boat were thought preferable to the dangers and difficulties of travel by road. Although Chaucer sent his pilgrims by land, even in his day it was just as usual to travel from London into Kent by two stages, taking a boat to Greenwich, Queenborough or Margate and then going on by road. The normal route from London to Greenwich was by the 'Long Ferry' and Canterbury pilgrims who weren't too hot at the walking or riding business could go as far as Queenborough by sea. By the seventeenth century we certainly hear that 'A Hoy from Rochester and Margate in Kent, doth come to St Katherine's Dock.' The rules of the Waterman's and Lighterman's Guild regulated this traffic. The Tilt boat, for example, normally used for the Long Ferry, had by regulation to be at least fifteen tons burden and have a canopy aft to give the passengers some shelter, while any waterman or wherryman wilfully losing the tide at Billingsgate or Gravesend was penalized. There were officers at London Bridge and Gravesend who had to attend at high water and ring a bell for fifteen minutes as a warning for boats to put off. Some idea of the extent of this river traffic can be gauged from the fact that at the end of the sixteenth century there were about three thousand watermen and two thousand wherries in addition to tilt boats, tide boats and barges. The Waterman's Company was an important source of recruitment for the Navy and as late as 1820 the number thus employed had risen to about nine thousand.

Round about this time the old Margate Hoy which, as you may remember was the subject of one of Charles Lamb's essays, was replaced by a steam packet and the Rev. Barham, author of the *Ingoldsby Legends*, who I can only assume had suffered on a cruise down the Thames could write of,

'..that best of improvements on boats since the Ark,
The steam-vessel called the "Red Rover", the barge
Of an excellent officer, named Captain Large.'

Sir Richard Phillips, editor of *The Monthly Magazine*, who tried this route to Margate in search presumably of copy, was enthusiastic about its safety. The packet had a 'band of music' to enliven proceedings and its speed was reckoned as six/seven miles per hour. In addition to the *Red Rover*, there was the *Marjory* plying between Wapping Old Stairs and Gravesend and the *William the Fourth* on the London-Whitstable service. Even the railway which was eventually to kill this type of water transport did not bring it to an end immediately, for the Canterbury-Whitstable railway, the first passenger carrying line in the world, was intended to join up with the water link from Whitstable to London.

The decline of river transport did not of course mean the end of Margate as a port; with the growing importance of holiday resorts it became a popular port of call for pleasure steamers plying between Southend and Clacton, though it was never apparently on the route of our old friend the *Medway Queen* (See *The Solent from the Sea*).

To Whitstable

We are not interested in Westgate-on-Sea and Birchington because they haven't got harbours and in any case we are now approaching one of the narrow sections on this route where the breakers which mark the drying edge of the Margate Hook are little more than a cable off and it is vital to spot the pairs of buoys, the Hook Spit and East Last, the Middle Last and the Horse which guide one safely through the tortuous channel. However, as soon as you are safely through, turn the chart over to 'herself' so that you are free to look at Reculver's twin towers. Reculver itself, the Roman *Reculbium*, is now mostly at sea and even the Church went in 1809, but by this time sailors throughout the centuries had got used to the towers as a landmark and they were saved by the intervention of Trinity House.

As to the origin of the towers you can take your choice. The humdrum historian is apt to attribute them to the surviving twin of two sisters who were wrecked off here when on their way to the shrine of the Virgin at Broadstairs. But if you are a discerning type with a nose for authenticity you may prefer to consult the *Ingoldsby Legends* again — where you will learn that the Brothers of Birchington were also twins, the good one a very devout Prior — and the bad one, of course, a dissolute Knight

'He drinks and he eats of choice liquors and meats,
And he goes out on We'n'sdays and Fridays to treats,
Gets tipsy whenever he dines or he sups,

And is wont to come quarrelsome home in his cups.
       No *Paters*, no *Aves*: An absolute slave he's
To tarts, pickled salmon, and sauces, and gravies;
While as to his beads — what a shame in a Knight!—
He really don't know the wrong end from the right!'

Now, as so often happened in the predictable twelfth century, the old 'Father of lies' who was taking a well earned siesta after a busy day, hears about the Knight, reckoned he had a candidate ready for collection for Limbo and sent Levybub to fetch him. There was only one teeny weeny snag, they weren't quite sure of the Christian name, but they felt this wouldn't matter much as they had a good description of their man even down to the 'little bald patch on the top of his crown' and 'a good Roman nose, rather red at the tip.' Needless to say as in all the best stories they collected the wrong man, Richard the Prior instead of Robert the Knight. In many families this might not have mattered much, but unfortunately for Old Nick, Richard was the blue eyed boy of St Thomas à Becket, who turned up in a fury, tore him off a strip and demanded to see Father Richard as well. In no time at all that worthy man 'began coughing, and sniffing, and sneezing' in a most lifelike manner. Meanwhile brother Robert had sobered up enough to wander in and was promptly whipped away and hidden up a chimney. Then the Saint really turned on the third degree stuff and got the devil frightened enough to disgorge his second prey on the grounds that the claim had been settled. Poor Robert, who had meanwhile fallen down the chimney, was picked up and given a good lecture by St. Thomas — enough anyway to persuade him to give away most of his property and retire to share a cell with his brother for the rest of his life. The only place he stubbornly refused to give up was Reculver and together the brothers built their towers to commemorate their happy escape — much more fun I hope you will agree — so nuts to the saintly sisters!

Whitstable

The old gentlemen with the forked tail must have had a soft spot for this bit of coast for I seem to remember he was also very busy about the streets of Whitstable. But first, unless we want to anchor outside we shall not be able to stay long here as it is a busy commercial harbour which has no room for yachts except those on a quick shopping expedition or clearing customs. Like all harbours along this coast it dries out completely.

Even in a fleeting visit you may see enough to feel that the older houses straggle rather untidily up and down the hill. Well, don't blame the Urban District Planner's Office, they can't help it because they are 'just as the devil dropped 'em'. They came originally from Canterbury which township the Devil had permission to destroy if the prayers at the tomb of St Thomas the Martyr ever stopped. After

Houses 'dropped by the Devil' at Whitstable.

being thwarted for years his chance came when there was too good a party during one festival and he flew in rapidly to pick up armfuls of the town. It only took him a few strokes of his wings to reach the open sea where he dropped his burden and went back for more. He managed just two more loads before an angel woke up the Sacristan and gave him the strength to ring *Harry*, the great bell which normally needed ten men to set it in motion. The poor old Devil was so shaken that he dropped some of his last armful on the hillside and divine intervention ensured that those which were saved were of the better type of house. The chart shows you this particular row of houses still on the spit running out to sea, the spit called Whitstable Street. It is said that certain awkward Antiquarians would have you believe that these houses are of Roman origin — what a pity the colour is going out of life!

The oyster industry at Whitstable is said to date from pre-Roman times. With beds on both sides of the Thames there have been recurrent complaints about poaching and in 1598 a petition was sent to the Archbishop of Canterbury complaining that,

> 'Certain seafaring men of Essex and other places have lately come hither into Kent, and there dredged oysters and caught great store of other fish, in the banks, sholes and streams and places of fishing near Whitstable and thereabouts.....And so is a great injury committed againt the old customs of that Kentish coast.'

Given the chance, the Whitstable men would retaliate and in 1725 the Southend dredgers claimed damages for the enormous sum of £17,000.

However, oysters were not Whitstable's only industry. It was an important port for coal brought down from the north by boat and loaded into trucks for the Whitstable-Canterbury railway. It was also, with Brightlingsea and Queenborough, a centre for the lesser known copperas industry, the clay, containing bisulphide of iron for subsequent conversion into green copperas, was loaded into barrels and sent up to London by water. This industry was flourishing from the fourteenth to the nineteenth centuries, so with the general river traffic the port must always have been busy.

The Isle of Sheppey

The importance of the Island of Sheep (the Roman *Insula Ovium*) guarding the mouth of the Thames, and its consequent attraction for sea born invaders seeking to establish a bridgehead, is obvious. Later, the Saxons were fairly thick on the ground by the seventh century and they had even collected about seventy-seven enchanting nuns by then, which they kept in a special abbey at Minster. The Danes, who arrived late as usual, had to make up for lost time and thought this was a very civil arrangement and with their unerring instinct, made straight for the nuns. Danes seem to have been an occupational hazard of Saxon nuns — or were they? A handsome Dane might easily have had the edge on a terrifying old trout of a Mother Superior — I wouldn't know! Sheppey has shrunk considerably, for Minster used to be in the middle of the Island. Anyway they had all disappeared by the time Hugh de Montfort took over after 'the Conquest' and was given military and civil command of the island, that he

'might the better guard the Thames and the estuary
of the river Medway.'

The dockyard was started and a small twelve gun fort built by Charles II as a defence against the Dutch. This of course did not prevent the Dutch from occupying it and sailing up the Medway, brooms and all.

One hundred and thirty years later Sheppey was to suffer one last invasion, though on this occasion it was not the French or Dutch but our own Navy. The Mutiny at the Nore in 1797 was a strange incident. A strong detachment of the Navy had been sent to Sheerness to protect the mouths of the Thames and Medway, but the seamen, who were already restless, were worked up into a state of mutiny by one of their colleagues, Parker, who named himself 'Port Admiral'. The ships all dropped down on the Nore and nobody was allowed ashore without a passport signed by Parker himself. He threatened to surrender to the Dutch, blow up Sheerness and sack Sheppey, indeed for a short time he and his mutineers were in command of the Island, parading through Sheerness under a red flag and generally creating an atmosphere of terror. After some negotiation, however, terms were offered which most of the seamen thought too good to refuse and the whole affair fizzled out with Parker having to be protected from his own seamen. There were two hundred arrests, but only the ringleader was executed.

These are but the bare bones of Sheppey's history. As you would expect, strange things could happen on the island. It was the sort of place which could keep a mock Hundred Court going until the nineteenth century and where St Bridget could get the Parson out of bed at midnight because a sailor, who had been buried next to her, plagued her with his grinning. Having dug up the corpse obediently, the locals then threw it into the river where it shuttled backwards and forwards between Sheerness and Gillingham Reach for the next few days. Subsequently, the Lord of Shurland got tired of seeing it whizzing past and ordered a reluctant parson to bury it again, whereupon he kicked the parson into the grave and swam his horse out to sea to collect a royal pardon — what goings on.

Much more in our own times, the Royal Aero Club opened a flying ground at Leysdown in 1909 for heavier than air machines. The Wrights, Moore-Brabazon and the Short Brothers were all familiar with this ground despite the fact that it was quite unsatisfactory, being cut up by drainage ditches. Shortly after Mr F. McClean (later Lt Col. Sir Francis McClean) bought an area at Eastchurch which he let to members of the Club at a peppercorn rent of 1/- a year. Facilities at Eastchurch and the loan of places were also offered to the Admiralty for the training of naval officers and from here the Royal Flying Corps came into existence in 1912 with Eastchurch developing into an important naval Air Station. Short Bros. built their first factory here.

R.A.F. pilots of the twenties will recall, I'm sure, the famous

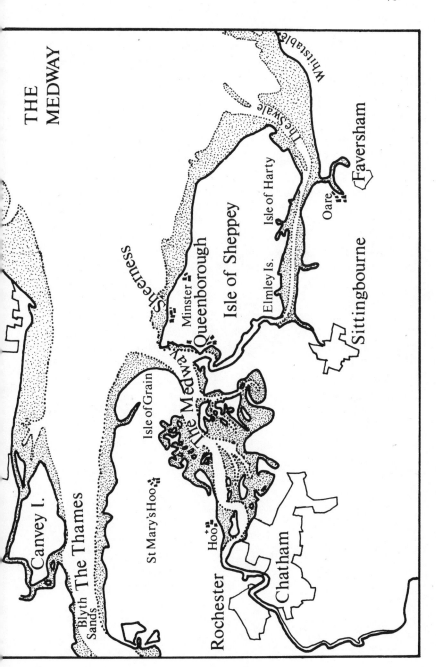

handicap race to Eastchurch village. The squadron was equipped with Fairy 3F aircraft but the pride and joy of the officers' mess was a much petted and pampered Old Aveling and Porter steam roller called *Buttercup*, as far as I can remember, because of her colour. She was proudly paraded most Sundays, but make no mistake she was no gilded   toy. Over many months, work went on tuning her up and polishing entry ports or whatever one does to steam engines until one day *Buttercup* excelled herself and attained, with a fair wind, the dizzy speed of 3.98 knots on the level. The time was ripe, it was decided unanimously, to pit her against one of the newer 3Fs — on handicap, I hasten to add! This was a delicate matter and called for many pints of beer in the mess because the discrepancy of speeds was of the order of some two hundred knots give or take ten or twelve knots. Eventually all was settled and the finishing posts established outside the village, just over a little bridge.

Now I don't know how many of you have raced a steam roller. Well, in case you haven't lately, let me say it takes about two hours to get a good fire going and steam up to 'racing pressure' plus a lot of oiling and general fussing round. Anyway, eventually *Buttercup* was under starter's orders and, with a defiant toot, away she went — thundering down the dusty road — with an anxious driver's wary eye on the sky behind. Just as *Buttercup* was breasting the bridge the roar of an aircraft engine was heard behind but over the hump, she got a second wind and hurtled down the slope to the flag — just two seconds ahead of the Fairy Fighter aircraft. *Buttercup* had justified the faith of the mess in her ability to make it. After that she was driven in a lap of honour round the village to the pub where she was given a long cool drink by her backers before being taken home in triumph to the mess.

I hate to finish on a note of sadness, but I have to report that the site of the aerodrome is now an open prison — which gives one to think!

The River Swale

But back to trivia; there are no difficulties in sailing round outside Sheppey, but it's rather more fun to go round by the Swale between the Island and the mainland. You have to time this passage because part of the Swale dries out and I would advise you to glance at Jack Coote's description of the peculiarities of these tides. Broadly, however, if you remember that the tide comes in at both ends, meeting somewhere between Fowley and Elmley, you will realise that you can keep a favourable tide most of the way round.

Though parts of Sheppey have rather lost their beauty by the creation of holiday resorts and caravan sites, here on this southern side it is still largely unspoilt marshy country. At the eastern end there is a good anchorage at Harty Ferry where you can get ashore on the north bank and visit the *Ferry House Inn* or the Tideway Sea Club in their motor barge *Charles Burley* moored off the South Ferry hard. Just to the east of Harty Ferry is the entrance to Faversham Creek and if you use your water there is time to get up to this pleasant old market town with its sixteenth, seventeenth and eighteenth century houses, on the tide and back again without having to spend a tide on the mud. If you are of really shallow draught you can anchor off the *Shipwright's Arms* at the junction of the Oare Creek, or on the tide go right up this creek to the boatyard. You will find the *Three Mariners* here and *The Castle* which does snacks and it is worth remembering that up an alley by the Harty Ferry turning there is a Post Office and shop.

About a mile above Harty Ferry the river broadens out into an extraordinary area of marshes, saltings and little islands. The channel is very narrow round about here, but it is so sheltered that you cannot possibly come to any harm if you do go aground on a rising tide. If you are in a mood for creeks you can go in through South Deep behind the bird sanctuary on Fowley Island and find your way up to the picturesque little Conyer Quay. There is also a good pub up here, *The Ship*. The Kent cherry orchards are said to have started up this creek, at Teynham. They were planted in Henry VIII's reign by Richard Harris who brought them back from Flanders.

After this, I am afraid the poor old Swale rather degenerates, as you come into the area of the great paper mills by Milton Creek leading to Sittingbourne and Ridham Dock. You will I think be a bit surprised at the size of the coasters which come up here by the twisting channel from Queenborough and keep your fingers crossed that you don't meet them on one of the worst corners. Once round the corner beyond Milton Creek there are no other difficulties, though you may have to wait for Kingsferry Bridge to open if a train is due.

Queenborough

As you come through the bridge the chimneys and cranes of the Isle of Grain will be appearing over the skyline, but long before you reach them, you will find yourself among the moorings at Queenborough. This is really one of the most sheltered and cosiest moorings in the whole of the Thames estuary but it is getting very crowded these days and you can't anchor anywhere near the fairway because of the big coasters going up to the paper mills that we have mentioned. With any luck, the harbour master will see you hunting about and will find you a visitors' mooring.

It is a strange place, Queenborough, it doesn't really seem to belong to this world at all. There is an eerie dreamlike effect about its deserted streets and the silent mud creek at the back. It resembles nothing so much as a film set for a Western that the company forgot to pack up when they left. It is tucked away round a bend of the West Swale, much as if it were a ranch town from the Middle West that was afraid of being discovered and swamped by the mad rush of Thames traffic swirling by only a few miles away in the estuary. The wooden pillars of the town hall and the oversized clock hanging out of the upper balcony all lend colour to this effect. However, you will find a pleasant pub on the waterfront after a quarter of a mile walk from the end of the hard which spans acres of mud flats. When we last rowed ashore there, four youngsters, who I think had been water skiing, were lying about in abandoned attitudes in the mud at the end of the hard, half under water with their rubber suits shining in the evening sun like so many porpoises. I can't help feeling that the modern youth seems to have odd ways of passing the time; but we chat and I find they have dropped their car keys in two feet of water and mud so we wish them luck and go on up to the pub, not only to drink but to fill our rucksacks with wine and spirits for the bilges. I remember the charming proprietoress explaining that her husband was up the creek — we gathered it was a habit of his at that time of the evening and she isn't very good at wines. However we give her a helping hand and unearth all sorts of good things. There's a cheerful garage mechanic and a young poacher who comment favourable on the lines of *Kala Sona* lying at her moorings. Oh yes, they have a boat but rather a lot of water comes in through the bottom and they point to a heavy clinker dinghy laying on the mud half way up the bank. The idea is that the water runs out again at low tide. They take part in the annual race round the Island of Sheppey but so far they have taken four hours longer than the next slowest boat. Last year, I gather, they got lost altogether and slept out in the open boat. It all seems the right spirit. Apparently the club thought so too because a prize has now been established for the longest cruise during the race and they have won it with unfailing regularity.

Well, I hope you enjoy Queenborough and that you find a

Queenborough still looks as if it was left over from a film set.

mooring. The shopping is quite adequate and there is only one village street so you don't have to walk very far. There is also a certain amount of boat building still going on up the creek at the back of the little town though this dries out at low water, and it is possible to get repairs done, if you go about it the right way. I shall never be surprised by anything that happens to us at Queenborough. There must be a sort of hoodoo on the place. Some years ago we looked in there on the way home from the Normandy coast and set off in the morning when there was absolutely no wind at all, thinking we would just motor up to the Blackwater, or if the wind got up, sail on to Harwich. But about two hours out, when there was still an absolutely dead calm, the little auxiliary petrol engine packed up altogether. Now it was an extraordinary day; it was the day of the seamen's strike for a start and all the big boys were crowding in to the Thames along the four or five channels from Scandinavia and round North Foreland so that at least the striking seamen could enjoy their strike in the comfort of the London port rather than being stuck out at sea. So it was a little like coming out of Brighton on an Easter Bank Holiday. Anyway the auxiliary packed up and after quite a bit of work done in the heat I traced this to the magneto which as you will agree is not the sort of thing you can repair at sea. Still no breath of wind and the echo sounder showed water just too deep for the length of chain we had. Eventually however, we did drift over one of the shoal banks and anchor at full scope. There we were, sitting in the middle of the rush of cargo boats into the Thames, praying for a wind. About an hour or so afterwards an extraordinary sight appears motoring slowly towards us. It was, I think a late Victorian or Edwardian river boat with a huge superstructure and what appeared to be about a foot of freeboard. I think they came over to ask where they were. Well, we could tell them roughly where they were and eventually suggested that if they were going into Queenborough which was about the best anchorage, they might like to take our line and give us a tow in behind them, the alternative being to hope that the anchor didn't drag towards high tide, before a wind came to our Rescue. So we opted to go in with them to get the magneto seen to and from there on – had a quite hilarious time.

Joan went aboard with a chart to show them where they were but it didn't mean a thing because none of the occupants had ever been near the sea before. The two young men turned out to be carpenters who were depressed by the prospects at home and had heard that they might make good money in Jersey. So, they decided to go there by sea and had bought the first available boat that they could afford. I think one of them had been out in a friend's boat once and the other thought he knew something about engines so they reckoned they'd be all right. It sounded all in good 'local boy makes good' British tradition. The two popsies they had with them were not so sure, as at least one had a vague idea the sea wasn't always like this millpond on their first day – she had heard it got a bit uneven at times; anyway as the traditional dumb blonde she was taking it all philosophically. The dark one was a much more entertaining character. She had married one of the carpenters the day before, having spent most of her life as a trapeze artist. Even so she was conscious that this was a curious way of spending a honeymoon, but at least she seemed to have got the domestic side organised; which was just as well, as the boys and the dumb blonde ate continuously.

Fortunately their engine kept going as far as Queenborough because there still wasn't a breath of wind. We had another drink and chat and equipped them with a few charts and a rough idea of what to do with them: and I made sure that they had a bilge pump which worked. We never did hear whether they'd arrived or not, but as there were no reports of motor boats lost in the Channel during the next two or three weeks we assumed that they made landfall somewhere — while we borrowed a spare magneto and wrote in the log — Queenborough to Queenborough, by courtesy of the *Princess Maud*.

The Medway

If you fail to get in at Queenborough your only alternative will be to run up the Medway, your nearest quiet anchorage being in Stangate Creek about two miles up river. Despite its width, this first reach can be a bit hair raising, with huge tankers manoeuvering to get in and out of the jetties and not always making their intentions clear to inoffensive little yachts. After that, you come to a wide no man's land of islands and saltings where, on a bad day, it would be only too easy to miss the buoyed channel before the river narrows by Chatham dockyard. Cockham is a pretty reach just below Upnor, but on the whole I find this river interesting rather than attractive. If you are a Dickens fan you can wander up the creek through the Hoo Salt Marshes to the village of Hoo with its memories of *Great Expectations* and, anchored in East Hoo creek for the night, you realise how lonely these marshes can be, even though you are cheek by jowl with one of the most crowded parts of England. You can indulge your fancy on this river with a choice of good pubs, such as the *Al Fiasco Due* at 14 New Road, Chatham where you will still get a delicious meal for a pound, the TSS *Arethusa* at Upnor, or a parcel of Norman ruins at Rochester. Indeed the castle which dominates the town and the river is a fine piece of Norman military architecture and the Cathedral nave is the oldest in England so I hope one or other of them 'turns you on'. The town itself, as befits its position at an important crossroads, is full of famous names. Chaucer stayed at *The Crown* (rebuilt about one hundred years ago); Shakespeare acted in the same yard and found it

'the most villainous house in all London road for fleas'.

Queen Elizabeth I also stayed here but left no comment on the beds, and Charles II seems to have preferred the *King's Head* — possibly a new barmaid.

With a fixed mast you will probably be unable to get through Rochester Bridge where the headroom is only twenty feet at M.H.W.S. and though thirty-nine feet at L.W., there is then only two feet six inches under you in places. In any case, though there is technically a further twelve miles of navigable water above Rochester, you can have it all with a bag of nuts, as far as I am concerned. Much of it is industrialised, the water in places is filthy with factory effluent, great baulks of wood are a permanent hazard to your propellor and tugs with long chains of barges are likely to come round sharp corners always in the most awkward places! But don't let me discourage you from having a go. After all we struggled on till just below where Hengist and Horsa fought their way to Aylesford though I gather even they didn't know what to do with it when they got there. And as every child will tell you, Dutch Admiral de Ruyter after taking Sheerness, sailed on up the Medway, broke the chain across the river at Chatham, took the flagship *The Royal Charles* and burnt six other large ships. It struck Pepys 'to the heart' even after a strong drink and Evelyn, journeying down to Chatham to see the Dutch fleet still anchored in the Nore thought it

'A Dreadful Spectacle as ever any English men saw,
and a dishonour never to be wiped off.'

Dutch sources, incidentally, deny the final insult that the Dutch flagship had a broom at its mast head.

The effects of this raid in London were, as you might expect, a state of near panic. Afraid that the enemy might come up the Thames next, ships were sunk indiscriminately below Woolwich to blockade the river. But what must have hurt that conscientious little man Pepys most was that the sunken ships were not just old hulks but included,

'The *Franakin*, one of the King's ships, with stores
to a very considerable value that hath been long
loaden for supply of the ships; and the new ship at
Bristoll, and much wanted there.'

The Dutch must have been laughing their heads off at these panic measures for I don't think they ever had any intentions of risking their own fleet up the Thames when they could watch the British destroying themselves and achieve all they wanted, a favourable

F

peace, by just blockading the mouth for a few weeks.

On the way in we didn't say much about the Isle of Grain. Have a good look at it, as you go back to the mouth of the Medway because I think it is a really fascinating nightmare world of cranes, tanks and twisted piping such as would make any futuristic film director drool. It's so messy it is almost fun, and yet within my lifetime much of it was as wild and lonely as Hoo Creek. There was even a port of sorts, Port Victoria, which still exists in name, though it is now rather swallowed up by the line of jetties and the outcrop of storage tanks needed by the huge oil refinery. Like Thanet, Grain is no longer an island.

The London River

Now I know a lot of people will snort when I suggest the Thames for sailing and if you are one, you can skip the next few pages. But, just as we explored the Essex Coast of the Thames in *East Anglia from the Sea*, I am going to suggest that the South Bank is well worth a visit. There is still much here that is of the very essence of old England, and of the once mediaeval highway, crowded with ships from the continent and later from the ends of the earth. And yet, to those who live on its banks it is also the village street, with the town hall and administrative buildings at one end and the open fields at the other, across which the track leads beyond the known horizon.

It is this intimacy between the City of London and its river that even yachtsmen who sail its waters must feel instinctively. The Thames is what the Tiber can never be to Rome, the Seine to Paris nor even the Scheldt to Antwerp; for none of these towns is a great national centre standing at the last crossing place, nor are the towns and rivers so interdependent as London and its river. The odd thing is that here the yachtsman really comes into his own because it is essential that you make the journey up the Thames quietly in your own little sailing boat and let the atmosphere absorb you. Arrive by liner or Southend pleasure steamer and the banks would slide by like some mechanised back projection, producing a eerie effect in a studio. You need time and the unhurried feel of sail to remember that most of what you are seeing on each shore was, until recent historical times, desolate marsh land surrounding a few islands of firm land which would take buildings. Plumstead and Erith marshes made one morass five miles wide and drowned twice a day until containing banks were built. Anyway let us wander up in case you are tempted to follow.

Sheerness to Gravesend

Tread softly, as you come out of the river because, as you probably know, that mess of masts and superstructure sticking out of Sheerness Middle Sand is the wreck of a war time ammunition ship, the *Robert Montgomery* which is too dangerous to destroy. The inhabitants of Sheerness have been waiting twenty-seven years for the big

Thames barges.

bang which the boffins predict will remove most of their roofs and all the glass! A bit of the front of Southend is expected to take off in sympathy. Now and then fishermen pick up bits of bombs that roll about but have so far wisely put them back. It is an odd relic and in spite of a forest of buoys, I have seen local motor boats taking happy sightseers between the masts at so much a trip!

Now I know this river can never have had the beauty of the

Seine with its lovely wooded slopes, because, as I have said, it was a primordial swamp before industry obliterated the charm of the few riverside villages. However I still find it both beautiful and exciting — in its own way. In the setting sun or on a day of great storm clouds, a skyline of factory chimneys, cranes and cooling towers can be both striking and of a singularly stark and compelling beauty. At other times when they emerge slowly from an early morning mist they have a dream like effect. Now, there are, of course, a few problems. The main shipping is less worrying than in many other busy rivers because there is usually enough water to enable you to avoid the main channel. But, oh brother, tugs are liable to come charging round a corner on the wrong side of the river if they are in a hurry and trying to cheat the tide, and without a powerful motor, you will have to moor to a disused barge or lighter during the adverse tide but you will always find something. In addition, there are a number of anchorages still in use and both Jack Coote and the P.L.A. *Guide to Users of Pleasure Craft on the Thames Tideway* are full of ideas. In any case the worst hazards are still baulks of timber which are a menace to a yacht's propellers and plastic sacks which fix you up more effectively still. This is why nowadays I would wait for daylight before motoring on the Thames.

Thames Anchorages

Gravesend

The first good anchorage on the way up is at Gravesend, where the 'Long Ferry' down the Thames used to stop. The 'Short Ferry' went to and fro across the river to Tilbury where the old Fort was built out to close the river in time of invasion. The right to run the 'Long Ferry' dates from 1402 and was granted as a monopoly to recompense the town for its losses after being plundered by the French. The price was fixed at 2d a head for a passenger with his bundle or at 4s for those who hired the whole boat.

Today, Gravesend is still important as the Headquarters of the Trinity House Pilots and the place where incoming boats for the Port of London are boarded by medical and customs officers. Before Trinity House was established by a merger of two Guilds in the early sixteenth century, the Pilots at Leigh had the monopoly of searching the inward bound traffic while Deptford searched the outward bound ships.

For the yachtsmen, there is usually space to anchor below the lock gates, but if wanting to stay a few days, particularly if the boat is to be left unattended while you go off to enjoy the delights of London, it is better to see the Club Secretary and ask him to find a hole for you in the canal basin. At one time there was a grandiose scheme for a canal from Gravesend to the Medway but the only relic left is a tunnel on the Gravesend – Strood railway which was built as part of the original canal link. I don't pretend Gravesend is a raving beauty but she is hospitable and trying to stage a 'comeback' in yachting – so why not help her out!

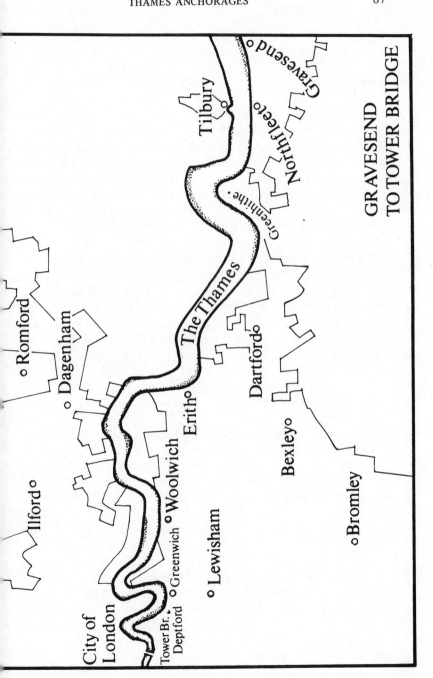

GRAVESEND
TO TOWER BRIDGE

Greenhithe

Greenhithe is, in many ways, more attractive and has the added interest of Ingress Abbey, but it is more difficult to anchor here. Anywhere along this Kent coast between Lewisham and Gravesend you may come across old chalk pits. For centuries chalk was dug out to manure the fields as well as being mixed with sand to make mortar. It was at Greenhithe that a new process was tried which led to the invention of Portland cement, but the most interesting result from all these chalk workings is in the parish of Swanscombe between Dartford and Gravesend. Here so much of the chalk has been removed that they have got down to the gravel below, revealing thousands of flint implements from early Palaeolithic times. There was perhaps more obvious fun in the Victorian days when the streets were full of vendors of 'Hot Eels and Pea Soup' and Mr Tiffin was plying his trade of official bug destroyer under a shop sign 'Tiffin & Son, Bug destroyer to her Majesty and the Royal Family.' He explained to Mr Mayhew,

> 'We can trace our business back as far as 1695 when one of our ancestors first turned his attention to the destruction of bugs — he was a lady's stay-maker.'

Kent is still full of odd occupations. I hadn't heard of the office of 'collar boy' until a few days ago. A young countryman mentioned to an old friend of ours that his father used to be employed to sit under the big table at Farmer's dinners and as each one slithered to the floor, his duty was to undo their collars and arrange them comfortably.

Woolwich

Above this there is no suitable stopping place until you get to Woolwich where Henry VIII's first dockyard was built, and even there, only if you can persuade the harbour master at the P.L.A. pier to fit you in. If, having worked out your tides, you hope for a night here I should give him a call in advance and you will be welcome — you may even, as we did, get a nice hot 'brew up'. It gets a bit disturbed here near high tide when the big ships are getting into the docks, but as compensation, it is fascinating to watch them manoeuvering.

Today we take the docks so much for granted that one forgets how modern they are. The first in London was built at Blackwall about 1660 and the next, which was later to develop into the Surrey Commercial Dock, at Deptford at the end of the same century. In 1805 we have the London Dock at Wapping with access from the Lower Pool and twenty-three years later St Katherine's just above it. Then there was a gap of fifty years until the Victoria and Albert dock was built in 1876, Tilbury ten years later and the King George V not until 1921.

As a matter of fact, until the second half of the sixteenth century there were not only no docks but also no 'Legal Quays' and in 1705 London's Quay frontage was only 1,419 feet compared with 4,000 at Bristol. The result was that most boats were moored in the river and unloaded by lightermen. With no control over mooring and at one time some 1,400 boats in port where there was berthing space for less than 900, the chaos can be imagined. This also provided a golden opportunity for pilfering. There were two main methods on record, apart from the activities of the coopers, watermen and rat-catchers. One was from gangs known as the 'heavy horsemen', men who were aboard legitimately unloading, but wearing special clothes with such capacious hidden pockets that they could take vast quantities ashore when they went off for meals three times a day. Their rivals the 'light horseman' were cruder in their methods. They just waited for nightfall when they would cut the richest ship adrift or board it by arrangement with the crew and pilfer it at their leisure. In addition to the horsemen there were the 'mudlarks' who would get aboard and just toss anything available over the bows into their little pulling boats.

Greenwich

I think most folk would agree that this is much the most attractive spot on the Thames below Tower Bridge. I remember motoring past in our little sloop one windless morning just about sunrise, when the stately buildings with their colonnades and cupolas fronting onto the river were reflected in the still water and framed against the background of its park crowned by the Royal Observatory. I won't insult you by recalling its well known history so let me just remind you that there has probably been a royal palace here since the time of Edward I and that, as you will remember if you watched the Six Wives of Henry VIII on Television, it was a popular residence for most of the Tudor kings. Sir Walter Raleigh chose a Greenwich mud pool for his celebrated cloak act with Queen Elizabeth. So, when you anchor just below the pier you can easily visualise that great host of boats that have lain here before yours through the centuries and the water pageants that set off from here as the royal parties moved up and down from London, for they would not have dreamed of going by road. Today there are two famous boats in dry dock here – the *Cutty Sark* and *Gypsy Moth IV*. You can visit both and I hope you will give my favourite little pub a call – I never remember its name, but it is straight across from the Maritime Museum entrance and first left. This reminds me that Greenwich village still has a lot of old world and attractive corners, which you will enjoy pottering round – perhaps after a visit to the Maritime Museum with its fascinating collection of old instruments, charts, books and pictures. It is one of the finest collections in the world and I would advise you to allow plenty of time to look around.

The Heart of London

Now, in case you have your mast in a tabernacle as we have, may I leave you with a last suggestion. It really is rather fun mooring in the middle of a large town, like Copenhagen, Amsterdam, Groningen, Dieppe, St Malo and dozens in the Mediterranean. But in England we generally find ourselves berthed away from the interesting and lively part of the town – in the dock area as at Dover. London is a delightful exception. St Katherine's Dock is not yet available for yachts though it won't be long, but meanwhile the P.L.A. will tell you that you are welcome at their piers – I could only wish they would say it loud enough for their Pier Masters to hear! We indeed tied up, after the exchange of small douceur, at the Royal Festival Hall pier and had a wonderful evening enjoying the lights and bustle of traffic across the water and watching London go to bed – from the river.

Sailing for Pleasure

I remember thinking that, so far as we know, the idea of boating as a recreation did not occur to anyone before about the seventeenth century. Then for a short time at least it became a royal pastime on this very river. Evelyn the diarist records in 1661,

> 'I sailed this morning with his Majesty in one of his
> yachts (or pleasure-boats), vessels not known among
> us till the Dutch East India Company presented that
> curious piece to the King; being very excellent sail-
> ing vessels. It was on a wager between his other new
> pleasure-boat, built frigate-like, and one of the Duke
> of York's; the wager 100 1., the race from Greenwich
> to Gravesend and back. The king lost it going, the
> wind being contrary, but saved stakes in returning.
> There were divers noble persons and lords on board,
> his Majesty sometime steering himself. His barge and
> kitchen boat attended.'

After this we hear no more about pleasure yachting, at least on the Thames, for about one hundred years but it may have been going on for some time for Fielding in 1758 saw some small boats sailing on the Thames and thought it would afford

> 'The highest degree of amusement to sail ourselves
> in little vessels of our own, contrived only for our
> own use and accommodation.'

How right he was, though even he could never have imagined how far the 'amusement' was to go in this twentieth century.

Envoi

Well, I remember thinking, as we left on the tide, at that magic
hour when you get the first perceptible lights of dawn reflected in
the water, that I had no regrets about the age into which I was born.
It is fun and fast moving and stimulating and yet it has not quite
severed its links with the past or lost sight of the eternal values; nor
have they been masked by the temporary assessments of each passing
generation. Man's belief in nature is continuous in the sense that his
desire to hold a mirror up to her is continous. It is the angle at
which he holds it that is all important and the thing that will deter-
mine his personal legacy to the next generation.

Indeed I finish this last book of our coastal wanderings with
one regret only, that I shall never sail from Limehouse Reach through
the Lower Pool in the early part of the seventeenth century — before
the great fire destroyed that old London of legend. I can think of no
more breath-taking Gothic skyline than the dozen or more spires of
mediaeval and Tudor London as they would have appeared as one
sailed into King's Reach on the tide. In the centre would be the great
majestic spire of old St Paul's cathedral upon its hill. It was famous
as the 'loftiest cross in Christendom' — far out-topping Strasburg and
Cologne or even the Notre Dame of Amiens. There was a city built
to enhance the landscape and at the same time make the most of its
surroundings. The spires have been replaced by domes and they in
turn by square box buildings designed as storage places for human
units. They and the streets are much wider and more sanitary — but
the other must have been breath taking, on a May morning at first
sunlight.

Bibliography

Pilot Books

The Cruising Association Handbook, Cruising Association, 1971.
Adlard Coles, K., *The Shell Pilot to the South Coast Harbours,*
    Faber & Faber, 1968.
Coote, Jack H., *East Coast Rivers,* Yachting Monthly, 1970.
Wheeler, Commander H.L., *The Pilots Guide to the Thames*
    Estuary, Imray, Laurie Norie & Wilson, 1960.

General Reading

Addison, William, *Thames Estuary,* Robert Hale, 1954,
Belloc, Hilaire, *The County of Sussex,* Cassell, 1936.
Collard, A.O., *The Oyster and Dredgers of Whitstable,* 1902.
Crouch, Marcus, *Kent,* Batsford, 1966,
Daly, Augustus A., *The History of the Isle of Sheppey,* 1904.
Finch, W. Coles, *The Medway River and Valley,* 1929.
Goodsall, Robert H., *The Widening Thames,* Constable, 1965,
Jerrold, Walter, *Highways and Byways of Kent,* Macmillan, 1923.
Lucas, E.U., *Highways and Byways in Sussex,* Macmillan, 1924.
Mais, S.P.B., *Sussex,* The Richards Press, 1950.
Mee, Arthur, *The King's England – Kent,* Hodder & Stoughton,
    1969.
Mee, Arthur, *Sussex,* Hodder & Stoughton, 1950,
Willard, Barbara, *Sussex,* Batsford, 1965.

Index